Unmarried Fathers

Unmarried Fathers

Dulan ⌐Barber

Hutchinson of London

Hutchinson & Co. (Publishers) Ltd
3 Fitzroy Square, London W1

London Melbourne Sydney Auckland
Wellington Johannesburg Cape Town
and agencies throughout the world

First published 1975
© Dulan Barber 1975

Set in Monotype Times
Printed in Great Britain by The Anchor Press Ltd
and bound by Wm Brendon & Son Ltd
both of Tiptree, Essex

ISBN 0 09 122130 7

For **Margery & Tony Parker**
with love and thanks

Acknowledgements

My first debt of gratitude is to all the men who talked to me, voluntarily and without recompense. Without them, obviously, it would have been impossible to write this book.

I have had invaluable help from the National Council for One Parent Families throughout. Although I must frequently have been a time-consuming nuisance, I was never made to feel less than welcome. My debt to the Director, Mrs Margaret Bramall, is truly incalculable. She frequently made a daunting task a pleasure. Her wisdom, warmth and insights guided me and any deficiencies in these pages are certainly not attributable to her or to the Council. In addition, special thanks are due to Miss Kathy Tither, who was endlessly patient with my queries and whose interest in the book was always encouraging; and to Mrs M. Cole Adams and Miss A. Duthie who gave me the benefit of their experience as social workers.

Mr Stephen Lloyd allowed me to impose on his precious time and answered all my fumbling questions about the law with great patience and kindness. I am most grateful to him.

Mrs Pauline Crabbe, Dr J. Lomax-Simpson and Captain R. Demery were all kind enough to talk to me and to give me the benefit of their experience. I am very grateful. I am deeply indebted to Reuben Pannor, Director of Casework and Research at the *Vista Del Mar* Child-Care Service, California, for permission to quote from his lecture, *The Unmarried Father – The Forgotten Man*, and from his, Fred Massarik's and Byron Evans' book, *The Unmarried Father*.

Last, but truly not least, I want to thank Paddy Kitchen for her faith, love and endurance in the face of my doubts and dramas; Giles Gordon for all his efforts on my behalf; Maureen Duffy for her criticisms of the MS., her support and tireless patience with my midnight phone calls; Philippa Harrison for her editorial guidance; Mrs D. E. Kitchen for her skill with the typewriter and her cheerful willingness to take on more and more work; Marjorie Lampard, who gave me some Monteverdi and Gesualdo in celebration; and all those friends, too numerous to name, who listened, enquired, gave me contacts and generally kept me going.

Contents

Acknowledgements   7

Preface   11

Part one   13

The Stereotype   15

The Interviews:

    Dickie: The good old days?   22

    Arthur: The most diabolical man in the world   30

    Ned: Your unmarried father personified   42

    Luke: An adequate day-to-day parent   52

    Boris: An eternal spectre of hope   67

    Andrew: Unmarried daddy   79

    Bill: A fortnightly father   93

    Peter: Future ways?   103

Part two   115

Introduction   117

The Unmarried Father and the Law   119

New Approaches to the Unmarried Father   136

Contraception and the Unmarried Parent   150

The Unconcerned Majority   169

Last Words   173

Preface

This book centres around a group of interviews with men who have fathered illegitimate children. The interviewees were contacted in various ways. Some answered advertisements (in the *New Statesman* and *Time Out*) describing the book and asking for help. Others heard of the book from friends and expressed an interest which developed into a willingness to be interviewed. One heard of me from an interested social worker and volunteered to talk. In one exceptional case, I read of the father's difficulties in a national newspaper and made the first contact myself.

Once contact was made, the interview was tape recorded and later transcribed by me. At no time did I have any contact with the women referred to in these interviews. This was an inflexible rule of my own making which was welcomed by the interviewees. It seemed to me unrealistic to expect a man to talk frankly about his relationship with a given woman – a relationship which was inevitably bad – if there was any chance of my passing on his views, information or whatever to her. I have tried very hard to keep details about the various women to an essential minimum. Their names and all other identifying details are, of course, false, and the same is true of the men.

In the hope of forestalling argument, it must be admitted now that these men are not representative of unmarried fathers *per se*. In spite of much that follows, the majority of men in this position do not feel concern, do not come forward to talk. Or, to be more precise, we assume that they feel no concern because they do not come forward. The silent majority, at least in this case, is assumed to be uninterested. Perhaps it is simply that their concern is private, or that there is no visible future in airing it. Perhaps social embarrassment is still an effective gag even in these outspoken and supposedly liberal times.

Whatever the reasons for silence, the willingness of my interviewees to talk about themselves as unmarried fathers sets them apart from the mass. Their willingness to talk indicates that they have thought about their situation, that it has exercised them in some way. These men also display concern in varying degrees. Even those who roughly approximate to the popular idea of an unmarried father – an absent, uncaring figure – are concerned with behaviour which now seems to them unsatisfactory. For most of these men, however, concern goes much deeper than that and is essentially directed towards the children. Obviously deep concern of this kind is likely to prompt a man to talk. Many of these men felt that by contributing to this book they might help other men facing similar situations.

I must stress therefore that I have not selected these fathers because of their concern. When I embarked upon the project I fully expected that it would be the distressed and the deeply paternal man who would contact me. I doubted that a representative of the supposedly uncaring majority would offer himself and I was right. I do regret his absence, however.

Finally, I believe that the unmarried mother and her child need and deserve all the help they can get. I do not accept, however, that this *must* be obtained for them at the expense of men or in the name and pursuit of their punishment. The woman who decides to keep her illegitimate child is grossly disadvantaged within our society. The improvement of her and her child's lot is a matter of vital necessity, but I do not think that this is likely to be achieved by harsher, punitive measures being enacted against men. In defending and discussing unmarried fathers, then, I do not intend to attack the unmarried mother. For considerations of space, it is not always possible to put her point of view in full. It has, in any case, been put many times before, whereas the fathers have not been heard.

Part one

'Unmarried fathers? They're usually considered to be such despicable people that the least said, soonest mended.'
DICKIE

The Stereotype

When I first mooted the idea of this book, it was greeted with general incomprehension. There was, I was told, absolutely nothing to say about unmarried fathers. Time and again discussion foundered on the assertion that the only interesting thing about out-of-wedlock pregnancies was the fate of the child and, I was reminded, the fathers were not remotely concerned with that. Even if I was right in insisting that there was a very great deal to say about unmarried fathers, I would certainly not find any such men who were prepared to talk to me about their experiences and feelings. In short, I quickly discovered that the majority of people have never given any serious thought to the unmarried father and therefore have nothing to say about him. Consequently, it is widely assumed that there *is* nothing to say about him. Beneath this simple equation I continually sensed a feeling that I was seeking to draw unnecessary and unhelpful attention to what one gentleman described as the 'embarrassing predicament' of these men.

It was something of a relief, then, to discover the work of Reuben Pannor, Fred Massarik and Byron Evans at the *Vista Del Mar* Child-Care Service in Los Angeles whose published findings have been invaluable to me. Social workers there had recognized that the whole problem of illegitimacy was influenced by the unmarried father and his relationship with the woman. They also noted that proper research into the role, influence and feelings of the unmarried father was long overdue. Their project had as its specific aim the involvement of the unmarried father in a casework relationship. They then hoped to determine from this what influence he had on decisions about the child's future, on the mother and how he himself was affected by this involvement. These comparatively simple aims were only achieved by detailed examination of a very complex situation and the published findings of the study* present a comprehensive portrait of the young unmarried father and his problems.

Of immediate interest to me was the fact that at the start of their researches Pannor, Massarik and Evans also met with a deal of scepticism.

Incredulity that an unmarried mother would consent to name the father of her child, or that he would admit to being the father, was expressed by lay and professional persons alike. They found it hard to believe that unmarried fathers would seek help from a social agency, or could even be induced to do so. Many were frankly sceptical that unmarried fathers had problems anyway; a typical observation was, it's the mother who's left 'holding the bag' – she's the one who is having the baby.*

This reaction is similar to that which greeted my own very different project and makes one ask why thinking about the unmarried father is so negative and so dismissive.

Firstly, we must accept that the unmarried mother's plight is obvious and immediate. The unmarried father can walk abroad without any visible sign of his paternity. It is easy to overlook him. The habit of a more liberal and helping attitude towards those who have violated society's norms, coupled with the emergence of women as a more or less equal creatures, have naturally helped to focus attention upon the unmarried mother. Far from explaining the lack of attention paid to the father, however, these factors only serve to measure how far thinking about him has lagged behind.

We can better understand the attitudes which breed this scepticism if we question the statement quoted above. Why should an unmarried woman refuse to disclose the identity of her baby's father? And once disclosed, or by other means discovered, why should the father deny paternity? The obvious answers are because society expects women to protect men, and because men are eager to evade their responsibilities. It will be objected at once that society has no such expectations

*Pannor, Massarik & Evans, *The Unmarried Father: New Helping Approaches for Unmarried Young, Parents* Springer, New York, 1971.

of women and that such a view of the male sex is cynical and, in a thousand particulars, demonstrably not true. Alternatively, it is sometimes suggested that women will conceal the identity of the father out of pride, in an attempt to prove that they can manage without the support of a man who has already rejected them. This is certainly true in some cases, but not as a generalization. It is again based on the idea of women as secondary creatures who must make the best of a bad situation and not 'bother' the superior male. Foolish and inaccurate as these attitudes strike us now, it requires little knowledge of social history to recognize that this has not always been the case. It is perhaps a fundamentally Victorian view of men and women and their roles, but then a great many of our moral judgements and expectations are still founded on essentially Victorian principles. Women were expected to protect men, their seducers, because men were all-powerful, socially and sexually privileged creatures. Men were expected to deny paternity for form's sake, and because knowledge of their pre- or extra-marital affairs could damage their social standing and career opportunities. They were, of course, expected to pay for their pleasure.

If this citing of outmoded social attitudes seems fanciful, consider these profiles of the unmarried father as reported by Pannor, Massarik and Evans.

When the father is thought of at all, he is often imagined to be an older sophisticate who has lured a young innocent girl into a compromising situation. Thus the mother is viewed as the victim of circumstances and is to be pitied. This lets every one 'off the hook' very neatly. No one except the amorphous father, unseen and unheard, is to blame.

Or perhaps the father is viewed as a sower of wild oats, and as such is surreptitiously regarded as having behaved in a manner that is to be expected of red-blooded youth. The woman who succumbs to his advances and becomes pregnant is then seen as one without morals who is reaping the 'just deserts' of her dalliance.*

I do not believe that the Victorian tone of this prose is accidental. Indeed, it is difficult to describe the common stereotypes of the unmarried father without recourse to such quaintly loaded works and phrases as these. And these descriptions

*Pannor, Massarik & Evans etc.

surely conjure up scenes straight out of Victorian melodrama. 'The older sophisticate' is the man of privilege who takes advantage of the innocent and economically underprivileged girl who is consequently 'ruined'. The 'red-blooded youth' is easily equated with the lustful young master and his companion in sin is the victim of an uncontrollable sexual passion. Both portraits are redolent of class and sexual privilege and set down coldly out of context they can only strike us as ridiculously old-fashioned and irrelevant. Yet they persist in the minds of many people and can only be based on cautionary stories learned at their mother's or more probably their grandmother's knees.

Similar stereotypes exist in this country, although I have found little evidence of the 'older sophisticate' type. He, it would appear, has been replaced by the married man looking for adventure. If caught out he is expected to remove himself, but the fact of his marriage is usually regarded as a pressure point by which he can be made to pay for his child. He is variously regarded as a fool, a calculating philanderer or a greedy seducer. The other prevalent stereotype is the 'red-blooded youth'. In the view of his elders he is often spurred on by the examples of a permissive society. His actions are often said to be the result of a general lack of discipline, respect for ingrained social taboos etc. His youth causes some to make allowences for him. There is a certain amount of peer-group envy at the deed and sympathy at his being caught out. However, he is expected to remove himself from the situation. His life must not be ruined by one mistake. He had best leave the field clear for the girl to become the focus of attention. In other words, the stereotypes on both sides of the Atlantic lead to a certain expected pattern of behaviour, the essential element of which is the man's disassociation from the problem.

The continuance of these stereotypes can in part be explained by another essentially Victorian phenomenon: a dual moral standard for men and women. With a sort of complacent despair our forefathers seem to have resigned themselves to the fact that, as far as sex was concerned, boys will and girls mustn't. This double standard still permeates society. Many of our expectations of the male can be traced back to this supposed fact of human nature and its all-important corollary that it is somehow 'all right' for a man to express himself sexually, but not for a woman.

In western culture the male is often regarded as a relatively free agent whose pre-marital or extra-marital indiscretions are, in some measure, tacitly accepted or overlooked. To say that unmarried fatherhood has been openly condoned may be an overstatement, yet it is not without its kernel of truth. We still place the major onus for out-of-wedlock conception on the girl. The boy is often subject only to raised eyebrows, if that, along with considerable *sub-rosa* approval of this proof of his masculinity.*

A similar view is expressed by Diana Dewar:
'The father has simply been proving his manhood in a way which is an accepted ancient tradition. The male seducer is an attractive figure of popular imagination: the seduced are fools, or simply wanton, or weak.'†

Implicit in our society is the idea that we want our daughters to remain virgins until they are married, and our sons to prove that they are regular heterosexual men. The onus to prevent conception is placed upon the girl because throughout childhood and adolescence she is warned to be on her guard against men who, in the nature of the species, 'only want one thing'. It is no good looking to the man for help, once she has given way. If she does not heed these warnings, then she must accept the consequences of her actions.

Similarly, boys are covertly encouraged to prove themselves sexually, yet must not be seen to do so. In exactly the same way we condemn violence while instilling it into our sons in the name of competitiveness and the manly virtue of standing up for oneself. The unmarried father certainly enjoys quite a lot of kudos. He has proved his ability to attract women, and has demonstrated his virility. But in conforming to one of society's expectations which, for once coincides with his own natural impulses, he also pulls down its wrath upon his head.

The position facing the unmarried father, particularly a young one, is consequently extremely bewildering. Under the circumstances his initial denial of responsibility is entirely understandable. It demonstrates not an innate selfishness, an

---

*Pannor, Massarik & Evans etc.

†Diana Dewar, *Orphans of the Living: A study of Bastardy*, Hutchinson, 1968.

eagerness to avoid responsibility, but blind panic in the face of impending rows, recriminations and the possibility of vaguely defined punishments.

Little is known, said or written about unmarried fathers because society expects them to remove themselves, even to run away from the situation they have helped to create. Thus it is fair to say that society has clearly delineated expectations of the unmarried father and that it brings considerable pressure to bear upon him to conform to them. They are: to remove himself from the scene and, if possible, to make financial recompense to the unmarried mother and her child. Beyond this he has no function save as an absent object of blame. Society offers no other model to the unmarried father and certainly does not take into consideration his feelings and problems.

In society's defence, however, it must be admitted that the exclusion of the father has a positive aim. It facilitates the flow of sympathy to the mother and it simplifies the immediate situation. There can be no denying that the presence of an involved father does complicate the situation. He represents a third opinion which the decision-makers have to take into consideration. Often they are ill-equipped, largely because unaccustomed and reluctant, to do so. His exclusion has the advantage of convenience, but is fundamentally unrealistic.

The law, which enshrines social attitudes to a large extent, is only concerned with the putative father's financial responsibility and here, at least under British law, some of the ambivalence which surrounds the whole question of out-of-wedlock pregnancies may be discerned. Legally, the onus is firmly placed on the woman who must apply for an Affiliation Order and prove paternity in the criminal court. Not only is this understandably embarrassing and distasteful to a majority of of women but, as many researchers have pointed out, it is scarcely guaranteed to encourage the father's responsible involvement. In America, there is considerable feeling that court proceedings actively alienate men. They view such proceedings as a threat and defend themselves by denying paternity. In other words, the scant legal machinery available to the woman to ensure the man's help often works against her and encourages his alienation from the situation.

In fact, of course, the legal attitude is essentially a punitive one. This strong punitive element can be seen even in reformist attitudes to the unmarried father. In her impassioned plea for the rights and plights of the single mother and the illegitimate child, Diana Dewar, for example, experiences difficulty in extending her compassion to the unmarried father.

Nor need sanctions against the defaulting unmarried father be limited merely to a threat of imprisonment if he can be found for trial and sentence. Perhaps some new penalties would help: he might be precluded from holding a driving licence or buying a house, or he might be declared a bankrupt. These are the kind of punishments which also deter because they would be approximately calculated to fetter a young man's enjoyment of life and some of its rewards while he refuses to honour his responsibilities towards the baby he fathered and forsook.*

These 'new penalties' are simply vicious acts of revenge which would do nothing to encourage a man to regard his child with affection or concern.

Elsewhere Mrs Dewar claims that the unmarried father is 'not always a villain' and is lucid about pressures brought to bear upon him. What she fails to make clear is how strongly these pressures act to make the man behave badly and how consistently society fails to encourage any other sort of behaviour.

The stereotype, then, is of a feckless, irresponsible, oversexed male. Society bewails the fact that there is nothing to be done with him – and never tries to do anything with him. It is against this model, which is the only one offered to most young males, that the experiences and attitudes of the following eight men have to be measured.

*Diana Dewar etc.

Dickie: The good old days?

Dickie is the only unmarried father I interviewed who remotely corresponds to the stereotyped view of such men. That, of course, is a blatant over-simplification, not least because Dickie is, by nature, non-conformist. It is a simplification worth making, however, because it shows how, when taken at face value, an individual case can approximate quite closely to the careless wild-oats-sowing syndrome. But, as Dickie is quick to point out, we are talking about events of nearly twenty years ago, and things were very different then. This, I believe, reinforces the irrelevance of the stereotype and demonstrates just how old-fashioned it is. Even twenty years ago it was essentially anachronistic. This is perhaps exaggerated in Dickie's case because he is the product of an anachronistic social machine. The scion – no other word so accurately conveys the relationship – of a rich upper class family, when asked about his background he says: 'Well, I was at Eton, actually, which probably answers most of those questions. I was simply sent there as a matter of course and it was a matter of course that I simply walked out again.' Largely in order to escape this straitening, predictable existence, Dickie became a prototype drop-out at sixteen, yet, in common with everyone else, he has not completely escaped his background. Today, his manner of speech and an admitted autocratic tendency remind one how strongly formative a person's background is. Dickie's unquenchable flippancy, however, cannot conceal a very serious and considered attitude to life and to individual responsibility. Yet as a young man I believe it is fair to say that he did in some respects conform to the only available model of unmarried fatherhood. Because of this he will probably be more easily recognizable as an unmarried father than many of the other men reflected in these pages. Yet it is, of course, his very individuality which at once illuminates and transcends the stereotype. 'One makes these mistakes and the only thing one can do is forget about them.' Not, as many will suppose, because men like Dickie are innately irresponsible and uncaring, but because life must go on for them as well as for unmarried mothers and illegitimate children.

BARBER: How many illegitimate children do you have?

DICKIE: Let me see. One, possibly two. I never was satisfied about my paternity of one of them.

B: Do you have any contact with them?

D: No, I absolutely don't. I don't think it's a very good thing. In the case of the illegitimate ones I don't even know where they are, except in the very broadest sense. I mean, I know what countries they live in, or did live in. I really have no further contact with them at all. In fact, in one case it was stipulated that her boy friend would marry her provided I never came anywhere near the home, which I thought was pretty reasonable, actually. So I never did. I've got a son by a previous marriage, but I don't interfere. I support, I maintain, but I don't have any dealings with them, or hardly ever, because I don't think that's a very good thing. I think it's better for a child to have one parent than two disputing ones.

B: Can we talk about the illegitimate children, in chronological order?

D: Yes, certainly. What little I can tell you. The first was in 1955.

B: Was this the result of a relationship?

D: Absolutely not, no. She was a girl I met on a beach, and we all came back to London. There were four of us: a friend of mine, another man, and myself and we met these two girls, had drinks at a nearby hotel and put 'em on the train, brought 'em back to London and sort of screwed 'em in the train all the way back. It was the Brighton Belle, actually. The good old days. Then we went round to my place and carried it on from there. Had a little party and things. Then we all sort of spent the night together. You know, it embarrasses me? Then I went abroad, where I was living more or less. I was away for four or five months. I came back and was told this dreary news. I was told by an intermediary. In fact, her girl friend, the one who had come up with us, got in touch with the man who was a friend of mine, and I heard it that way. Rather a long way round. I never actually saw the girl again.

B: There was no pressure brought to bear on you?

D: Pressure to stay away. Pressure not to go anywhere near, simply on the grounds that the boy friend said, 'I will accept paternity of the child providing this dreadful man never comes near either of us again.' And of course it was a tremendous let-out for me. I felt pretty bad about it, needless to say. But I don't think she did. I mean she seemed to have the child, from what I could understand, perfectly normally, and that was that.

B: The boy friend was around before you came on the scene?

D: Oh yes. She was going steady with him. Unfortunately, she was forced off the straight and narrow by us. He may have been, perhaps, a dull, pedestrian sort of fellow. I don't know, I can only speculate. And she got bored with him, one fatal day and a night and that was it. All I know is that the child was a girl. There was no other message received from that day to this.

B: What about the second child?

D: Well, that was when I was living in New York. I became very friendly with a Negro girl and we had an affair for quite some time. But I do know for a fact that she was having affairs with a whole lot of other men as well. She was very keen on white men. I was very pleased that she should be keen on white men. . . She told me that she was pregnant by me, but I knew two other boy friends of hers. We'd all kind of had her. So I wasn't at all sure that I was, necessarily, the father. But she never insisted. She never made a thing or a fuss about it. She wasn't that kind of lady. She was an easy-going, extrovert personality. In fact, I think she wanted to have a baby. She took no steps to get rid of it or anything like that. Well, I then married somebody else, while the coloured girl was pregnant. She went home, and that was that. I didn't see her again. Rather sad in a way.

It was just really casual sort of intercourse, you know. Very casual in the case of the English girl. A single series, all within the space of twenty-four hours. And the other girl, over a period of some, what, two months, I suppose. It's hard to be sure about time, now. It was such a long time ago. I don't know what the Negro girl did about it, whether she had the child finally or not.

B: What about your marital status?

D: Well, I've been married three times. My first marriage only lasted sixty-three days and there was no child. My second wife I had a child by. Then I married my third wife, who is my present wife, and we have a child together. I married my second wife, actually, because I got her pregnant. I thought, well, I really can't go on... This is ridiculous. Like a fool. I should have persuaded her to have an abortion, or something. Except that she wanted the child so badly. The child was six months old when that marriage broke up, when I broke it up. I do go in for short marriages, yes. Well, when you marry people you don't know... I suppose I'm much keener on my work than fostering relationships.

B: What do you feel about children now?

D: You shouldn't have them if you're not prepared to look after them. This is step number one. Nowadays it's much easier to be like that because the girl can be on the pill and no pregnancy need ever result. I criticize myself very strongly for not having made these women have an abortion. I had no money at the time, which didn't help very much. Where was the £150 coming from, or whatever it cost? I'm going back to the fifties now. Abortions were really the rich man's get-out then, but they weren't really available to society at large. However, I suppose having got an illegitimate child, or a child as a result of a broken marriage – there's really very little difference, except the illegitimate child's even more confused, doesn't even know what its name is – you're in the hideous position of having to decide according to the circumstances of the particular situation whether you're going to do better to go on seeing the child, or whether, having got out, to get right out. The only rider is, where there's no material hardship involved, which there wasn't in my case.

B: What about contraception?

D: My responsibility resides in the fact that when I was very young I never used to practise it.

B: Why not?

D: I don't know. There was no time, or one was suddenly taken with a tremendous urge to screw the person, and vice-versa, and one just thought, Oh well, hope for the best. Because, as I say, in those days, there was really very little alternative. There was no pill. I've never worn a french letter in my life!

B: Why not?

D: Oh, I don't know really. There was never really one at hand when I wanted it. I mean, you can't say, 'I'll just pop down to the pub, to the machine to get a Durex or something.' I just never happened to have one there, you know? And of course it spoils your fun which, in those days, was all I really thought about. And actually, to do myself justice where I can, I think the girls did too. The girls certainly went in for contraception far more. Dutch caps and so on. But they were pretty fallible, either because they were put in wrong, or were the wrong size, or everyone was in too much of a hurry. I worked out that I had to procure at least thirteen abortions. It was pretty nerve-racking, actually, in those days. You had to go to psychiatrists. It was all a fiddle.

B: It still is.

D: I'm sure. Mercifully, I've got past the stage where I have to bother about it. It's all pretty disagreeable really, you know. Flagrantly bent and completely unnecessary.

B: Did you have any contraceptive training?

D: Good heavens, no! Absolutely not.

B: What about sex education?

D: None. None at all. Especially not at school. I just went out into the world and put two and two together. The army, actually. Not that we were ever given any sex instruction there, either, but most of the blokes had already had it. I think that was the first place where I came up against sex more or less solidly, because the conversation was never about anything else. You can imagine, with eighteen hundred men cramped up in a barrack. But then I was very highly sexed when I was young and thoroughly enjoyed screwing. Never felt guilty about screwing. Sex was an escape from the feeling of guilt I had had in other directions.

B: Do you ever feel guilty about having brought illegitimate children into the world?

D: Yes I do, actually. I feel sorry . . . I mean I think the world's a terrible place in its own right and I think, therefore, if you can't start a child off with a reasonable material chance, then better not start him or her off at all. I do definitely feel that. In a general sense I've always had doubts about having children on the grounds that the world wasn't a safe enough place to put them into, and I get really very cross with people one can see have children because they know it's the thing to do. The chattel impulse. I do feel bad about it at times.

B: So that if you had your time over again ... ?

D: I'm forty-one now and much less turned on by the whole thing. I'd probably do the same thing all over again because I'd be the same sort of person. I've often been told I was very irresponsible, but funnily enough it wasn't that. It was a question of trying to find out for oneself – because nobody else had bothered to tell you – what responsibility really meant in these areas. Since they never told one what it was, one simply had to try to find out by creating situations. I won't say it was as conscious as that but I think, looking back on it, that was obviously what I was trying to do in a somewhat eccentric way. Sort of suck it and see, really.

B: Do you think children should be given comprehensive sex education?

D: Definitely. I entirely agree. I think the thing to do is to instruct them about the pill and other contraceptive methods, and also about VD. That's important because it seems to be on the increase. There's something very peculiar, I'm sure, about the sex education that is meted out to children even now. Behind all this liberal façade there is still something terribly stuffy, oppressive, old-fashioned and even perhaps religiously oriented. Actually, one should be taught to think rather than sex education, or indeed any sort of education. One should be taught to use one's brain, because everyone's got one.

B: Do you think your public school background, sexual ignorance etc., affected your attitude to women? Were you frightened of them, for instance?

D: I felt immediately drawn to women. Certainly never saw them as frightening. You meet the occasional frightening woman. . . I've been much too fond of them. That's my trouble. Actually, I have a rare blood group which apparently results in very fertile sperm. When I was young I practically only had to look at a woman and she was pregnant. I once had a sperm sample taken and they said, 'Oh God, no wonder you had a bit of bother.' It's just one of those irritating things. I remember the first time a girl told me she was pregnant my feeling of absolute shock. I was terrified, actually. I thought, What on earth am I going to do now? Find an abortionist. What's an abortionist look like? I can't look him up in the phone book. All these problems are associated with the problem. It wasn't a girl I remotely wanted to marry, or who wanted to marry me. Something had to be done. Well, in the end I had to help myself, quite honestly. That was a dreadful experience. It put me off sex for a whole week.

B: A whole week?

D: It really was absolutely horrific, actually. At least it horrified me at the time. It was very competently done, as it happens. He simply said, 'I'll have to have someone to help me. You'll have to have it done in your flat. There's nowhere else we can do it.' I had to get rid of the two men I shared the flat with for the week-end. I'd never have got rid of them if they'd realized what was going on. I had to invent all sorts of excuses. Aged aunts coming to stay – anything to get them out of the place.

B: But you presumably stayed around? Was that a fairly shattering experience?

D: I had to actually help and then see that she was all right afterwards.

B: What was that like?

D: Well, it was all right, I had the most extraordinary desire to screw her again. Absolute lunacy! I didn't do any such thing.

B: But the idea crossed your mind?

D: I was so amazed by the effect of just performing this simple act. I was only, what, about twenty-two. We were very young at twenty-two in those days. It was amazing really.

B: How did you find an abortionist by the way?

D: I happened to have a male friend who'd been through this experience and helped.

B: And since you didn't want to marry the girl concerned, did it ever cross your mind that she might want you to?

D: Yes, it did. First of all I thought, How ghastly! Her of all people. Luckily it turned out that she had no such plans in mind. Mercifully. I would have refused point blank.

B: What if one of your illegitimate children turned up on the doorstep one day?

D: Well, I don't know. I'd say, 'Come in, have a drink.'

B: It doesn't fill you with terrible foreboding?

D: Oh I don't think so. It would all depend on what his or her attitude was, I think. I mean if it was a minatory attitude I should react sharply, but if it was a benevolent attitude, I would sort of be genuinely curious. If I thought he or she was going to try and blackmail me, or anything like that, you know, say 'I'm going to go round telling everybody', I'd say, 'Go on. Have fun.' One's attitude would be dictated by their attitude, really.

B: Finally, do you think there is such a thing as a paternal impulse?

D: Oh yes, I would think so. Whether it's a good thing or not, I don't know. It depends on the individual, of course. I definitely think there is such a thing. Once people can function in a reasonably stable environment, normal people will automatically feel paternal feelings and want to do the best for their children and take a great interest in them and so on. It's pressures that distort natural impulses, you know. External pressures cause internal ones.

B: Well, thank you for talking so frankly to me.

D: So many people know about my little peccadilloes that I really don't mind telling you.

B

Arthur: The most diabolical man in the world

'It seems to me customarily taken that the unmarried mother is always the poor girl that's been victimized by the man, and the man's got out of it and is going to enjoy himself. Even Joan's brainwashed with the fact that if I'm now sort of a single man I must be going out enjoying myself. The fact that I'm possibly eating my heart out. . . What I want is something to do with my son; something that we have produced, not me, *we* have produced him, and that's been taken away from me and there's nothing I can do. She will get all the sympathy even if she happens to be a thoroughly bad lot.'

Arthur looks a lot younger than his fifty-seven years. His clothes and general appearance remind one more of a wiry stable-hand than an office worker. He is loquacious, despite the laboured breathing that testifies to the recurring chest complaint from which he suffers. Basically his story is a simple one, but it is complicated to a degree in the telling. He has an almost obsessive need to make himself absolutely clear and to be fair to Joan, the mother of his illegitimite child. Thus almost every statement he makes about her, the situation, and especially his feelings, produces a string of qualifications. Throughout he draws a fine distinction between the unvarnished recollections of events and his various 'theorizings' on them. His speech is telling precisely because of its circumlocutions, hesitancies, underscorings and contradictions.

It is essential to understand that Arthur's awareness of himself as an unmarried father provides a focus around which he can describe his general state of confusion. Sometimes one suspects that he would seize on any classification, put himself into any pigeon-hole, so long as it provided him with a temporary means of defining his problems. This is not to say that he is in any way insincere in his feelings for Brian, his ten year old son. In fact, this recent and sudden discovery that an unmarried father is a man virtually without automatic rights over his child is particularly poignant for a man of fifty-seven who has enjoyed twelve years of reasonably happy common-law marriage.

The difficulty in describing Arthur is that his type is generally overlooked. He represents the grey, undramatic side of the working class. Probably his greatest problem is that he is undeveloped as a person. An innate intelligence seems constantly to be at odds with stereotyped expectations and standards. Hence the contradictions in his story and his reactions. If there is a guiding principle in his life, it is probably that he will do almost anything for a quiet one. He opts out of difficult situations, but always for what seem to him to be the very best of reasons. This trait is compounded by his liking for strong, uncompromising, but not notably purposeful women, who leave him confused and reeling. Above all, he is a man who needs somebody to talk to.

'I suppose I was naïve about women. I've always got on well with them. I like female company, but I'm not a womanizer. Put it that way. Talking to a Nigerian who works here with me now, and telling him all about our affairs, he just said, Well, I didn't understand women. And even women have told me that. I can't understand the mentality of women. And this Nigerian bloke, I mean, the things he's told me about women! He's more of a womanizer than I am. And I've come to the conclusion that, in some cases, some women, if you ever try to figure it out from their point of view, you'd just never understand it. What seems commonsense and sequence to you, may not be to a woman, and nothing will ever make it so.'

Arthur delivers two interwoven monologues. One describes his life – particularly his relationship with Joan. The other concerns Brian, his son.

Arthur met Joan, a married woman with three children, five years after his first wife had divorced him for adultery. 'We done seventeen years and had three daughters.' His reaction to this latter event was to cut himself off from his 'former family' and completely change his life-style. He had not thought of settling down again, but Joan threatened to commit suicide if he left the town where they met without her.

Because of their age – Arthur was then over forty, Joan several years younger – they decided against children, but Joan changed her mind and Brian was born. For eight years they lived happily and conventionally as a family, but then Joan got the first of three 'uprisings', as Arthur terms her restlessness, involvement with other men and, latterly, sexual indifference.

The first of these events was a short-lived and relatively unimportant infatuation. The second had more serious reper-cussions because Joan left Arthur, taking the child with her. Again she was infatuated with a man, but nothing came of this relationship, and she returned to take up a job as a housekeeper near to the home she had shared with Arthur. After a while, they patched up their differences which, at that time, seem largely to have consisted of practical matters.

Joan resented the fact that, during her absence, Arthur had altered his will entirely in favour of Brian, but he changed it back again. Also while she was living away from him, Arthur discovered that her husband had divorced her, and he broke this news to Joan. 'She was insistent that we were to get married which I was happy to contemplate because it would legitimize Brian, apart from anything else. But it wasn't convenient to do it right there and then.'

However, Joan appeared to be willing to give the relationship another try and they had, in Arthur's phrase, 'a grand reunion'. As far as he was concerned this was to be essentially a sexual reunion. Because of Joan's job there was no opportunity for sexual relations, so they went on holiday and Arthur fully expected that their sex life would recommence. He was totally disappointed, and when he tackled Joan about this, they quarrelled.

Arthur accepts that Joan is undergoing the menopause and

has made efforts to understand the difficulties women experience at such times. This knowledge only seems to increase his sense of women as incomprehensible, inconsistent creatures.

'I think I'm a normal man as regards sex. I will talk about it and I enjoy a certain amount of sex, but I have no perversions. I just like straightforward sex, with variations, as far as myself and Joan are concerned. We didn't seem to have any trouble in the first eight years. She was as keen as I was, but in the last couple of years it's been a case of, "Oh, that's a filthy subject," unless she was in the mood. "Oh, no, no, don't talk about that. It's dirty. I'm not interested." Yet if she felt in the mood she'd be just . . . Which seemed to me so inconsistent.'

For a while the relationship drifted on in an unresolved state. Although still living apart they were in regular contact and Arthur wanted Joan back. She, however, would not commit herself. When I met him, he had not telephoned or seen her for a month.

'The only difference this time – I don't know if you fully realize this – it's myself who's made the break. My wish would roughly be that we could be reunited. The fact that I know it is practically impossible ever to attain that doesn't alter the wish, although if she does come back, I'm afraid I'd have to say, "No, Joan, I can't chance any more. There's been too many occasions where the promise has been good, but it's not been kept. What guarantee have I got for the future?"

'I'm being selfish there. I took the first one very badly. I got to the stage of going to the Samaritans. I've been to the Samaritans on one or two occasions. Unfortunately, if I take a little more drink than need be, I get into the mood where it isn't worth it all. I have a stack of tablets which I keep on one side, and every now and again I toy with the idea . . . Although I'm beginning to master that now, because it's a stupid thing to get into. But at times I've got so low that I've thought, "I'm not going to make it. It might be my fate." I've been very successful in my life in many ways, but I haven't been successful as it were in my love life. The first one I blew up myself. This second one, which I put such a lot into, because it came late and so sort of out of the blue, and produced a son and seemed to be so perfect . . . I began to think, is there another hurt around the corner?'

Arthur is punch-drunk. He had obviously settled completely for a life with Joan, but her two 'infatuations' have left him insecure and confused. He wants her back, yet he cannot believe that she will stay. He suspects that she may be using him as a convenient 'doormat' until another relationship offers itself. He lacks the resolve to abandon her entirely himself. He veers continually between a conviction that the relationship is now definitely ended, and a romantic hope that she and Brian will return.

'We always greeted with a kiss, even when this silly state was going on. When she met me she would offer herself to me and kiss me which, you know, made it seem crazy. But of course I was, and possibly at this moment still am, very emotionally involved with her, and she isn't with me. I think it would seem that she has infatuations with people that go for so long and then they suddenly die and that's it. Because it was like that with her first husband. Her husband was the most diabolical man in the world, but I've since realized that he probably wasn't because now I am the most diabolical man in the world.'

I have given only the skeleton of the story which, quite apart from being well and truly fleshed out in the telling, runs parallel with musings about Brian. He repeatedly says that Brian is rather backward, that he is disturbed and hostile, particularly towards his mother. He admits that he has no idea what goes on in the child's head, but he is sure that he has been harmed by the unsettled state of affairs between his parents. There can be no doubt that Arthur misses his son and grieves about him. 'Probably there will be no quiet moment during the day when I'm not thinking of her and Brian.'

At the same time, Arthur has always steadfastly refused to make any financial provision, except by affiliation order. His reason is that only in this way will he get tax relief. Since Joan never actually got as far as this, although she has been advised to do so and Arthur has no objections, he pays two pounds a week into a deposit account. 'That as far as I'm concerned, is maintenance for Brian.' Similarly, when I asked if he had ever tried to talk to Brian about his feelings as a result of recent events, Arthur immediately offered a detailed list of excuses.

'No, Brian's never spoken to me about the time she took him away, although I used to have Brian of a week-end, when they

first came back. He used to come to me about twelve. I'd prepare a nice lunch. Then she'd come and we'd go out shopping
or whatever. She'd stay the evening until about nine o'clock. I
then escorted her home, either by taxi or walked her home.
Brian would be looking at the television, and then time for bed.
In the Sunday morning it was a case of getting up and doing the
odd chores, having breakfast and then getting ready to go up to
Mummy at dinner time. So we never had a lot of free time in
which we could sort of browse around, and so I never knew much
at all about his past.'

These are just two of the anomalies in Arthur's account of
his feelings for his son. More than anything they reflect the
confusion of responses and feelings which seem to be the one
constant in his character. In all fairness, however, it must be
noted that they are only occasional interruptions in a monologue
of pain and self-doubt.

'Now he's an unusual child. I've seen many indications. For
instance, not so long ago we got talking about things, and I
forget how we got on to it, but he told me, or he was expressing
a fear that he would be left. I said, "What do you mean?", and
he said, "I think I'll be left on my own." I said to him, "No,"
I said, "of course you won't. Your Mummy loves you and so do I."

'I told her about this but she dismissed it. But it was very
significant. A boy of ten had in his mind that his mother, or
that *we* would leave him. Now I, in a sense, have left him in so
far as she had taken him away. So that covers me. I've left him.
He's right. Now her, I believe her behaviour when she was away
had made him reason that perhaps she might suddenly fly away
and leave him. Whether the child was justified in thinking that
or not. . . It was a thought.

'I could never interfere with Brian. If ever Brian's schooling
came up. . . because he appeared to be rather backward, and
I'm rather an impatient sort of man, I used to try to coax an
answer out of him. It seemed to me that she would always come
in on it and sort of over-ride me, and in the finish I'd just retire
and do nothing. But then she'd throw back at me that I wasn't
interested in my son. Well, I ask you, if I had three daughters
and Brian would be the only one that would carry on the name,
my thoughts for Brian, even if they didn't appear to express

themselves, was always for him and to do everything for him, even if I couldn't do the conventional things. I don't know. I possibly could be criticised on these lines.

'Apparently when she left me that time, Brian was beginning to show hostility towards her and she knew it would become a problem, so she approached to the school authorities that she'd want some assistance in controlling Brian. So this social worker comes on the scene, but the bit that astounds me is that none of the social people as she's had on her side have ever approached me. And that's what I can't understand. Surely there must be a complete picture?

'I'm reluctant now even to go to the social people because without the cooperation of both parents. . . But whoever I go to they would have to make an approach to her. First of all I don't think she would possibly take it up, and secondly, I've got the point of view, well perhaps they wouldn't be all that concerned if it becomes, as it were, a hopeless case. Well, why bother?

'What I'm sort of wishfully thinking about is if her problems with the boy are so great she might be prepared to approach me purely on that basis, and we can get something sorted out that I can have Brian. And if that works out, it'll be all right.

'I think he's a child that possibly takes after me. I'm terribly sensitive about things and I'm thinking that he probably feels the same way, but he bottles it up inside him. All I hope for now is that when he gets say eleven, twelve, thirteen, fourteen, when he gets more worldly himself, if he wants to come and see me, he will come and see me and we may eventually have a happy reunion.

'The very last time I saw him, Brian was playing about in the garden. He was sitting on a stool, looking into space. I waved to him from the house and he eventually saw me and waved back, but I thought to myself, he was sitting there thinking, a ten year old boy. You know, didn't even come down to the house.

'She came back to see me and Brian went across the back gardens to a neighbour's place. She said, "You'll phone me, won't you?" I said nothing. "You'll phone to find out how we're getting on?" So I said, "Well, I'll see." So she kissed me goodbye and left.

'Now Brian never came to say goodbye, which was sort of unusual. So I don't know whether he was stopped, or whether his state. . . that he forgot. I haven't actually seen Brian since that point.

'Any time that I've seen the child, to wit this business when he was sitting up the garden, it hurt me inside to see the boy like that because, to me, a child should always be happy, and it pains me to see a kid like that. Even if I'm inadequate enough to supply what he needs, I think, well, why can't I supply it? A child is not just something that is a product of half an hour's pleasure.

'Now I claim that I have all the feeling in the world for Brian, but perhaps I don't show it to other people in the physical sense, and they feel justified in saying that I haven't got feelings for Brian. Perhaps, basically, I haven't. Obviously, I'm mixed up. I don't know whether I'm coming or going. To a certain extent I've been brainwashed. I only feel what I say about Brian, but do other people see that I'm so twisted I don't care about him? Believe me, I've been part brainwashed sometimes to the extent of thinking perhaps Joan is a hundred per cent right, that she couldn't be with me, that I'm that bloody bad. . . I get to this question: Could I be so mesmerized by myself that I think I'm right and correct but everybody else can see that I'm a diabolical individual?

'There's absolutely no thought about the boy, you see. That's the bit that galls me. I cannot even approach her on these lines and say, "Look, what about Brian? Why shouldn't we be doing something for Brian?" She takes this hard-line attitude. "Oh, I'm the one that should do it all." Now she absolutely mothers Brian. Every move he makes. "Brian, don't do this. Brian don't do the other." And Brian has been, well, he's not a normal ten year old boy that should be dashing and flying around. She's battened on to him so much that she's making a proper ninny out of him. I don't think I'm being unfair to say that. Brian's only got to go out of her sight. "Brian? Brian? Where are you?" So Brian has got no guts or confidence. And I've seen that going on and I could do nothing about it. I can see the boy possibly being part destroyed through her attitude, and there's nothing I can do about it.

'Within the last few weeks, before we finally broke up, he played a day's truant at school. She never knew exactly where he went on that day. He claims to have gone to London Airport on his own. Knowing Brian, I don't think it's true. He doesn't know that I know, so I've kept it dark from the boy. But she was going to find out, but I doubt whether she ever will.

'And before he went away, apparently he left a note, saying, "I'm going to America, Mummy, but it's not because of you." Why the child should say that I don't know, but she doesn't pursue it. She was going to sort out this problem on her own. She was going to see the psychiatrist at school. But her attitude wasn't, well, *we* will. . . It was *her* that was going to sort it out. All the time it's telling me to keep out.

'As I say, I've had no contact with Brian in the last month. I don't know what I'm going to have with him in the future, it's still uncertain and I don't know what might happen. She might make a contact by letter or phone or physical appearance. I might not see her again, but as far as I'm concerned I'm not going to make any move at all, apart from giving Brian his Christmas present. I've got it for him, but it's too large to go through the post. Now the condition between myself and Joan is such that I cannot be sure that if I deliver to the address where she is now, it would be accepted if she knew that it came from me. I also suspect that she may be propagandaing the boy to be hostile to me. I can't sort of get around that one.

'In actual fact I think I can solve the problem by actually meeting the boy from school and passing the present to him. It's not a heavy package, although it's big. He would be able to carry it. If I confronted him and said, "Here you are Brian. This is your Christmas present, not to be opened until Christmas," well, then, she couldn't, I mean unless she was completely diabolical, do anything about it.

'When I made this break I was going to have Brian there and just say, "Any time, you can come to see me," but I didn't do that. I waited until Brian had gone to bed and she only heard this on her own. Now I haven't seen or heard of Brian since and I can only assume two things. Either Brian is so nonplussed about all that has happened, he's taken the view of saying nothing and asking nothing. On the other hand, he may be asking to see Daddy and she would very well say, as I theorize, "Your father has dropped us. He doesn't want to know. Unless we have a telephone call from him, we'll never know." So I'm absolutely tied really, to do anything about the boy.

'I haven't seen her for a month and I propagandaed myself into believing, now this is all over. It's got to be all over. And yet I find that probably there will be no quiet moment during the day when I'm not thinking of her and Brian. What's going to happen to Brian? How is Brian taking it? What is Brian's future going to be?

'I would like to have him at least to come with me part of the time so that we could just sort of grow up together, so that he could sort of know me, and I could assist him. He's obviously going to get interested in all sorts of things as he gets older. I'm interested in electronics and mechanical things in general and if he was to show interest in these subjects it would give me great joy. To think of making something together would be just marvellous. Even if it meant that we're not going to come to-gether again, but to have contact with him. . . I don't want, if possible, to be divorced from him.

'My problem is with Brian. What I can do with him, or what I can't do with him. I don't know. You see, I don't know who I can go to officially now, in any way. I don't think I'm far out by saying that Brian must be suffering in many ways, but what the the hell can I do for him? I don't sort of want to take him away from his mother. I don't want it to be a case of, "You come to me. Your mother's no good," or anything like that. That's why I'm taking this attitude of retiring out of their life, doing much the same as I did with my first family.

'He might get a bad impression of me, but when he's old enough to reflect on what was said and done, if he's got any faith and feeling for me, he will say, "Well, I want to see my Dad." And if it happens to be in another three or four years' time, when he knows what he wants, I also know that I would never tear his mother apart. In a way she's to be pitied for being so, in some ways, stupid to herself. Because she must have a hell of a prob-lem with a boy that's growing up and has been a problem. I've seen him get very hostile to her, very hostile. Yet, if you met him outside, you'd think he was a mouse. But to us, particularly her, he's been diabolical. And, of course, she'll think nothing of thumping him. When he gets big and old enough, who knows what he might do to her? He might start to knock her about. I I hope he doesn't, but he might even do that.

'I should never, at any time, like to sacrifice Brian, whatever the conditions were. I basically feel that we brought him into the world, as it were, under rather unusual conditions. He was decided upon quite willingly by me and her, and having produced him, I certainly wouldn't want to sacrifice him in any way whatsoever.

'If he wants me I'll give him all the help in the world. If by any chance he grows up and he doesn't want to know me for whatever the reason may be, well, I'll have to bear that and put up with it. But I personally would like to have him and do all that I can for him.

'Now I lost my father when I was sixteen and it's always been a great source of regret that I never had a father. So I am thinking the same thing of Brian. Is he going to say, "Where is my father? I want my father?" So he can have me. It would be the greatest joy in the world to have the boy grow up to be something, to see him mature into a nice young man. I'd feel, well, that it's all been worthwhile. He's not just a body, he's part of me.'

The most poignant and disturbing aspect of Arthur's situation is the helplessness he feels now that he is forced to consider himself an unmarried father. Of course, it is not true, as he maintains, that he has no rights whatsoever concerning Brian. If he went to court he would very probably be granted access to the boy, much as a divorced man would expect to receive. But this is not Arthur's way. Not only is his instinct to opt out, 'to do much the same as I did with my first family', but courts are frightening, expensive places. Besides which, to take such action would be to admit that his relationship with Joan was over and the options closed. Sadly, he has little faith or trust in social workers. He feels that they tend to take sides, particularly Joan's, while she has steadfastly resisted his wish to consult a marriage guidance councillor who, he thinks, would be impartial and act as a channel of communication between them. In fact, as we have seen, Arthur is beginning to regard his problem as a hopeless case.

Hopeless or not, it pinpoints the unnecessary difficulties which face the unmarried father. These difficulties have grown up simply because he, the unmarried father, has been overlooked. Now that we are slowly beginning to acknowledge his existence, even to the point of encouraging his involvement in the situation, it is surely time to give him a few simple rights in the matter; rights, moreover, which are automatically available without recourse to the law. The very atypicality of Arthur's situation actually reinforces this argument, for there is a considerable number of men, whom we should perhaps more accurately term 'common law fathers', who may one day find themselves totally cut off from their children, simply because, like Arthur, they never got around to marrying the mothers of their children.

'I'm a bit of a romantic. I mean, any happy ending to anything is something I thoroughly enjoy. It doesn't matter what it is. I can never agree to anything that hasn't got a happy ending, which is, of course, fairy story stuff.'

Ned: Your unmarried father personified

'I was born in 1944. My father was in the services and my mother was living on a farm. I am the youngest. When the war was over, my father took a post in Africa, as a District Commissioner, and the family moved out there and the next five years were spent living a very wild life in some quite remote places, going barefoot a lot and speaking native languages. Came back to England when I was seven and was programmed through the preparatory and public school system. I could never come to terms with the amount of external discipline that was imposed on one. I left school when I was sixteen. I did a number of things. Eventually I started travelling, and working for an American company. Then I decided that I wanted to go to the States, so left and went there.

'My father went abroad again shortly after we returned from Africa. My mother and he were divorced. She married a wonderful person, but he died. You could say that the background I've had, from a family point of view, is very much a broken home environment.'

Ned is not his chosen name. The one he chose he described to me as his 'alias/assumed/spiritual name'. He has a mid-Atlantic accent, a legacy of the years in America, and a curious trick of repeating the first phrase of a sentence two or three times while he formulates the rest. Sometimes the accent is accentuated, re-inforced by vocabulary to evoke the mid-late sixties, Haight Ashbury, acid trips, rock music; a time when it all seemed to be coming together and about which young people are already beginning to feel nostalgic. It was against this sort of background that Ned met and made pregnant an English girl, Margery.

'If it hadn't been for the fact that I had a sort of instinctive repugnance towards contraception, Amy would never have been born. What I basically did was I cut a hole in a contraceptive. Now I don't mind. You can use this. Now I don't know to this day why I did it, I know how much joy Amy gives Margery, anyway, and it's very far out. Margery was the one who wanted me to make love to her, and she wasn't too worried about the whole concept of using a contraceptive or anything else. And I remember I was. . . It's very difficult to know how to explain this. It's probably inexplicable. . . I remember at the time really wanting to have a child. It was incredible, if you stop to think about it. Yeah, personally, man. This is in many ways incredibly selfish when you look at it, but when you consider that we did live together for three years, it's perhaps not quite so selfish. I literally cut a hole with a razor blade in a contraceptive. I didn't do it every day. No fanatical process about it. I was in the bathroom one time when I was fairly stoned and I remember thinking how damned stupid the whole thing was, and I did this thing and it's as a result of that – I mean it's a million to one shot when you stop and think about it – that Margery became pregnant. I never told Margery that. I never told anyone that. It was a weird thing to walk around with in your head, man.'

He married Margery before his eldest daughter was born and two years later they had a son. His detailed account of this marriage and its break-up is a story of growing incompatibility. Ned became more and more involved in the drug culture, Eastern religion and philosophy, progressive music. Margery accused him of being a hippy and, at least potenially, a drug addict. Things came to a head when Ned discovered that an ex-boy friend had sent Margery some money so that she could return to England whenever she wanted. He left her and was immediately charged with a drug offence. 'She wasn't prepared to use the money she had towards my defence, so she returned to England.' Shortly afterwards, Ned followed her, literally skipping the country.

'I was suffering a heavy psychosis effect from all the acid I'd done the year before. Call it paranoia if you like. Call it what you want. But what I wanted was a woman or a person who was spiritually in the same place, state of conciousness as I was. I didn't need anyone who was going to attack my mind in any sense of the word. What did worry me was that every now and then I'd really miss the children. I obviously wanted to be with them without having to go over and see her relatives and what have you. I went over there one night and brought them back and later on Margery came back with a policewoman and her sister all hysterical, and they took 'em back again. I ended up being committed to a mental hospital for a twenty-one days' observation period. I literally sort of just freaked out. Not violently. I didn't harm anyone. I didn't steal anyone else's things. I just thought, Well, all this is nonsense, the whole thing is absolute nonsense, and I felt very resentful, too, towards a lot of people who'd been singing a lot of wonderful things on record, yet not being aware of the pain they were creating.

'She came down to see me once after I got out, and I was pretty messed up because they'd given me electrical shock treatment against my will, but my will wasn't broken as regards one or two spiritual ideals that I was holding on to and which had brought me into the whole area anyway. We saw each other in the park and there was a vast, vast gulf between us. Shortly after that I moved down to Wales. It was about three weeks later I got a letter from Margery saying I'd be surprised to know that she was back in the States. She divorced me. She put the proceedings through in the courts over there and divorced me for total incompatibility.'

Ned has not seen Margery or his children since the divorce. After a spell with a religious community, he joined a commune for a while before moving on to Ireland. In another commune there he met the girl who was to bear his illegitimate child.

'It was at this community that I met Sarah. Sarah at the time was seventeen and she had just literally left school and had thrown in her lot with all these strange people.

'The community life is quite an exacting sort of life and I was quite committed to it, actually. I was called the Guru, which was a name I didn't ask to be called, but that was the name they called me there. I had one or two small confrontations with authority, the police department. The community did as a whole, but I handled a couple of them from the spiritual approach, totally. That was alien to them and they didn't know how to react. It was very successful.

'I tried to keep myself as much as I could free from any binding relationship, or even making love to any of the people at the community purely as a means of physical sexual release, you know? What happened was that it became very obvious to me that Sarah was extremely interested in me as a person, and was singling me out. So we naturally began to spend a good deal of time together, talking. After a while she showed me a lot of poetry she'd written. I know that's a very usual development, but it was very profound poetry and in many ways it was like the other half of a realization.

'I was jailed for twenty-one days for begging for the community and when I got out Sarah and I started off from a different point of view because she suddenly started to see the other relationships I had with other people. This created an even more profound link between us in terms of actually being able to speak very openly and honestly about anything that we were going to do. It became very obvious after a while that we were forming a very strong relationship at all levels of the word.

'We got talking very naturally about the whole concept of making love, having children, and I told her that if we did make love I would want for us to have a child. "So if you don't understand that," I said to her, "then don't make love. Don't sort of lead me on, or involve me. As long as you realize this, well, that's great. Let's have a child. Let's do the whole thing. But until you're ready to accept that, then let's just stay where we are now." She was astounded at the honesty of my saying a thing like that, because a lot of the other people were only involved in terms of the whole one night stand concept.

'So we decided to go to England and I think it was then, really, that we decided that we did understand the importance of being fully here now, as two people, and that we did want to have a child. It was a tremendous, total commitment to each other. Still is, though it's changed shape now. So I told her I was very into Krishna consciousness, and still am. I'm not a good example of it, necessarily, but I am into it. I told her that the whole concept of a child is deepened if one starts to think in terms of the body as purely a container, a means by which a spirit, a soul, an entity, a being may manifest in the earth plane, and that the sort of thoughts that one perhaps projects into the ether, into the realms of consciousness, attract beings, entities that are already in existence. Children aren't just brought by the stork, so to speak. This was something that was very natural to her. She just accepted it very readily.

'She didn't accept that if we made love we must have a baby immediately, because she didn't understand. I had to introduce her to other people who did understand, which I went to some great pains to do, so that she could see that I wasn't just saying this to trap her, or to secure her in any way whatsoever. She did understand it because, don't forget, she was listening to a lot of music and beginning to understand a lot of music. Some of the concepts in it, especially in some of the West Coast music. . . She understood very thoroughly.'

Returning to Ireland, they discovered that there had been an attempted murder at the commune and, Ned says, talking to one of the victims who lay at death's door, helped Sarah to understand more fully.

'He believed in the transmigration of the soul. He believed that he had lived previously in this plane and he might live in the future in this plane, and when Sarah saw him literally at death's door, talking in this way, she began to understand even more fully and thoroughly, because he was talking about his next birth. So she discussed this with a friend of hers quite fully, because this girl found that she was pregnant and decided that she wanted to have it aborted. So I explained this whole concept that children aren't just sort of extensions of yourself, and gave her a few booklets on it, too, actually, written from an Eastern point of view. And that changed her mind considerably. She called her son by my name. I don't know if there's any coincidence.'

There followed another trip to England, Sarah was now pregnant and Ned again fell foul of the drug squad, this time in Scotland. He was about to re-join Sarah, who had preceded him to Ireland, when the police picked him up in Wales.

'So I was taken to the police station in Wales and held for three days. Then I was taken off to Scotland and brought before the court and put into prison for observation. In vain I tried to tell them that Sarah was two months away from having

a baby and what this really meant to me; that I hadn't got time
to go through this observation; that I was guilty of smoking it,
so please fine me or sentence me or do whatever you're going to
do very quickly. But they held me in prison for twenty-one days.
I came up before the court again and there was an eclipse of the
sun. That was rather strange. They then remanded me to a
mental hospital, in a closed ward, for further reports. So I tried
to explain to them that this was all absolute nonsense, and that
my wife was going to have a baby. "Your wife? You're not
married." "Well, all right then, she's my common law wife."
"Common law? What's that?" They didn't want to acknowledge
the existence of anything like that. So I told them, "Unless you
people take some course of action, I shall escape." (And they all
thought, Well, that's the talk of someone who's round the twist
anyway.) Well, I chose my moment carefully, and I did escape. I
literally took the law into my own hands.'

Back in Ireland illegally, he took a job with a tied cottage in
order to make a home for Sarah and the baby.

'They wouldn't let me be present while she was actually
having the baby, although she wanted me to be. They were very
specific about it. Her own name was written on the card, and
all the rest of it. Their reactions towards an unmarried father
were quite interesting. He should have been hanging his head
in shame in a good Catholic country. Hiding round the back
and here he was right in there every day, so to speak.

'And I got in there about half an hour after the birth and
actually was the first person, apart from Sarah, to see that we
had a girl. Sarah said, "What shall we call her?" and I said, "Well
what do you think of Angela?" It was just a name that came to me
on the spur of the moment. And she liked it, so there it was. So
before her parents or the priest or anyone could arrive on the
scene, we had already chosen the name for our daughter.'

After Angela's birth he lost his job and was picked up by the
police and returned to Scotland. He now faced two charges:
the original one of possessing cannabis and a second of trying
to defeat the ends of justice by escaping. He was held for seventy-
one days before trial and then fined for the first offence and
admonished for the second. Sarah and the baby joined him in
Wales again, but they soon decided that they wanted to live in
Ireland.

'We rented a cottage and lived there right through the winter. I started doing quite a lot of work for Divine Light Mission. Sarah didn't get into that at all. She was taken up, obviously, with Angela and that immediate scene, but I had to get into it quite heavily. She wanted to get married. She said to me she'd like to get married in bare feet. I said I didn't know about the whole idea of marriage because it was all so hypocritical. I said I didn't know what sort of priest I want pronouncing rites between us. I mean I know some people on the street who could do it more profoundly. No, she didn't specifically want a Catholic marriage. It was just that she wanted the concept. She wanted to express this sort of spiritual desire to appear in a sacred place, with no shoes on, to make the moment more profound for her, and to have someone pronounce something tangible between us. Something tangible that she could relate to.

'It wasn't that I didn't want necessarily to marry her, and was outraged by the concept of being married in a church. It wasn't that at all. It was just simply that I believe that it's not for the love of a wife that a wife is dear, but that it's for the love of the soul of a wife that a wife is dear. And she does, too. She's been very intimidated by the orthodox point of view, by an orthodox establishment. As far as I'm concerned it has already been solemnized and Sarah will really realize that – on one level she totally realizes that and accepts that. It's only this question of it filtering back to her parents, and mine, too, gradually. As far as Sarah's parents are concerned, I am Angela's father, but it is up to me to establish a position of security, then their respect for these ideals and concepts will become a material thing that they can relate to.

'It will come right, but it won't come right from an orthodox point of view. The important thing is that Angela sort of grows up in an atmosphere which is free from any quarrelling, or any fighting, or any sort of tugging over her. Sarah is very anxious that – obviously now that Angela's getting older – that Angela starts to identify with me as a father-figure, but she's not sure how she's going to bring this about. And the answer is that she's not going to bring it about from the position she's in because she's in a hopeless position. She'll want to live with people of a compatible outlook and no matter where she goes and looks for that sort of life-style, she's always going to be missing something if she knows that she can't give Angela to me for a few days. She's also very aware of the fact that I've been through a good deal more than she has in terms of just actual tension and confrontations with the establishment, police departments and judges. Well, this whole thing is in the process of coming right – coming right is a strange word.'

The relationship at this point was inconclusive. Ned was in England, Sarah and the child with her parents in Ireland. There were hints of pressure from both his and Sarah's family that the position should be regularized, if only in terms of Ned providing a secure home and making financial provision for them. This he talked of doing, but in the context of his own spiritual pursuits. He wanted to set up a spiritual centre which would, if he succeeded, incidentally provide a home for all his children.

Shortly after that meeting, Ned sent me seven foolscap pages entitled *Unmarried Fatherhood* which provides some interesting footnotes to his narrative.

'In accordance with Divine Inimitable Laws, which I am forbidden to transgress, her mother and I made it possible for this "entity", "being", "spirit/soul" who is our daughter to take the physical body that resulted in the union of her mother and I. . .

'I do not believe in the use of those things that make it possible for a man and a woman to consummate their sexual union *without* LIKELIHOOD of bringing an embryo into the womb of the mother'.

In the original text, the word 'fear' stood in place of 'likelihood'. The word had been crossed out and 'likelihood' substituted in block capitals.

There follows a repetition of events surrounding the child's birth, his prior imprisonment etc., and an admission that his relationship with Margery – 'She was a woman who could never have been faithful to one man' – was an absolute failure.

'In the case of Angela's mother, Sarah, there was never any question of "success" or "failure". If Sarah had not had Angela by me, it is entirely certain that she would have given herself to anyone else who wanted to make love to her and give her a child. You must understand that it was a *baby* that Sarah wanted, not a husband, not a permanent relationship with *one* man. She specifically made this clear. And I got hurt. She remained aloof and proud.'

This, of course, does not tally with his other statement that it was he who insisted that if they made love, Sarah must accept the possibility of pregnancy. If her desire for a baby was so great why did she require so much persuasion before committing herself? If she was so specific about not wanting a husband, are we to understand that Angela's birth made her change her mind? There is a hint here almost of their roles being reversed, of Ned making the greater emotional committment and being hurt. This, incidentally, is his only reference to being hurt.

The last sheet of this communiqué is headed *CONCLUSION* and reads as follows:

'As a direct result of having become a father separated from his first two children for well nigh four years by eight thousand miles of land and sea – And as a result of having also become an official unmarried father separated from my youngest child by the very rifts in our society/isles that are causing the strife in Ulster and now Eire – narrow-minded sectarianism, propagated by quiet fanatics of TER-RORIST ORGANIZATIONS

'I have decided that the past no longer matters to me. I am only interested in the present and building a brighter future.

'All warfare is wrong – I will not ever be ashamed of being a father – no matter how great the criticism of my enemies.

'My friends do not criticize me – some of them find themselves in similar situations.

'TRUTH AGAINST THE WORLD: UNMARRIED FATHERS OF THE WORLD UNITE.'

Many people will find it easy to dismiss Ned as a drop-out, a hippy and a drug-addict. To this last charge I must point out that he is not an addict. He spoke honestly and voluntarily of his use of LSD and cannabis resin, but he mentioned no other drugs. His manner and behaviour throughout our meeting was definitely not that of an addict. Nor is unmarried fatherhood, as far as I am aware, a symptom of hippydom.

Experts who have worked with drug users often maintain that these people are searching for something, a sense of purpose or fulfilment. Religion, as we know, fulfils that need for many and I believe that the incidence of a connection between the use of soft drugs and the embracing of Eastern religions and philosophies is too frequent to be insignificant. Then again, psychologists have suggested that the fathering of an illegitimate child can provide a similar sense of belonging, of identity and fulfilment. Ned's experiences, therefore, may represent such a quest, conducted on three fronts. Each foray presents him with an identity, hence his description of himself, in his first letter to me, as 'your unmarried father personified' and his fondness for the slogan, 'Unmarried fathers of the world unite.' Nor should we overlook his strong desire for a child back in America when he cut a hole in a condom.

Perhaps the deliberate act of fathering Angela should be regarded as a considered attempt to proselytize for his spiritual beliefs, for a more honest world based on love and peace. Yet it is equally possible, particularly with regard to Sarah's desire for marriage, to see this as a classic case of illegitimacy, with all its attendant problems. Certainly it brings into sharp focus the conflict between the Establishment and an Alternative Society. Spiritual and religious convictions are of no use in solving the day-to-day problems of raising a child. That burden falls on conventional society, in this case represented by Sarah's parents, and so the fires of animosity are fuelled. Some will see Ned's spiritual convictions as a convenient means of avoiding what society would call his obvious responsibilities. These beliefs are sincerely held, however, and may ultimately provide the security he apparently lacks, but in common with all religious convictions, they tend to create at least as many problems as they solve.

Luke: An adequate day-to-day parent

'I remember once, during the summer, I went to the Social Security Office and said, "Look, I want some money, for myself and for my son." They said, "You're a man, you have to register for work before you come here, then you'll get a cheque. You haven't got stamps, so this is the only way we can do it." I said, "No. Think of me as an unmarried mother, because I am the same." They had to make this shift and yes, they did make it.'

The family is 'upper to middle class', involved in the creation and teaching of art. They are liberal Catholics. Luke is the eldest of three children and regards himself as more fortunate than his sister and brother. 'I benefitted from their being overlooked.' Like many eldest sons, he enjoys a special, close relationship with his mother who, with considerable justification describes him as 'an unusally charming person'. He is the very apple of her eye. In addition, Luke has an unshakeable respect and admiration for his father.

The girl in the case, Joyce, is working class, but the confusion of her background is so labyrinthine as to resist analysis. She is herself illegitimate, apparently disturbed and with the bastard's sadly common lack of identity and secure emotional orientation. She drifts, periodically, into petty criminality and seems unable to cope without the support of a man, even though she frequently rejects this.

They met when Luke was sixteen; Joyce was two and a half years older. Luke was enrolled at a further education college to take his 'A' levels. He soon ceased to attend, however, and began to frequent the local art school while living in a 'ramshackle and undefined commune'. When he met Joyce, he was looking for sexual adventure whereas she was 'in need of emotional support', having just left her husband. This affair also coincided with the temporary estrangement of Luke from his mother.

'I remember one time, which I regard as a very important juncture, was when my maternal grandfather died, and my mother was extremely upset. I was fourteen or fifteen or so, and I went up to help her with dealing with her mother, and dealing with the funeral. She was obviously acutely feeling the loss of her father and she opened up all her anxieties, her anxieties of her life, to me. I was not really ready for them. I was very shocked to think of my mother having affairs. . . having an affair with her tutor when she was a student, and having affairs after she'd been married and so on. I think it was a mistake of hers to have made these sort of confidences to me, at that time. I think I was rather shook up about that, and I was resentful of her. I went through a phase of not having enough respect for her. I didn't regard her with respect and there was an estrangement. . . I don't know what it was because of, but it certainly coincided with my affair with Matthew's mother. I can't think of any other actual, positive reason why I should have been estranged from her, other than this taking me into her confidence and using me in a role that would have been more suited to her husband, really. . . It simply occurred that I ceased to communicate with her.'

Luke himself places significance on this coincidence of events, and perhaps they do, in part, explain a relationship which is crucial to an understanding of Luke's personality. Superficially, his estrangement from his mother looks like a classic rejection once the idealized mother-figure has been sullied and lessened in young eyes. The really important aspect of this situation, however, is surely his awareness of being placed in a role more suited to a husband than a son. Luke was, as he recognizes, the last person who could help his mother through this crisis, yet her appeal seems to have awakened the impulse to help, if only by making him aware that older and supposedly more capable people had confidence in him.

Without this element, one would expect him to seek out an

identifiable surrogate mother-figure. Joyce was scarcely that, but her relatively greater age and her considerably greater experience as a married woman should not be overlooked. Nor should the fact that these are qualities which define the ideal mistress for many young men. Yet I am convinced that the clinching factor in their relationship was the 'high state of emotional tension' Luke says she was in when they met. This afforded him the opportunity to play the husband, the supportive male role to a distressed woman. Having failed to help his mother as he must, given the nature of that relationship, Joyce provided him with a chance to prove that his mother's confidence in him was not misplaced.

In a curious way, this also indicates the unusually high level of his maturity. Few boys of sixteen are prepared to shoulder the emotional problems of an older woman, but he increasingly felt a responsibility for Joyce and his developing emotional involvement with her was certainly based on the belief that he could help her. And, of course, she was in much greater need of help than his mother, as subsequent events demonstrated.

This sense of responsibility undoubtedly crystallized when Joyce followed him, penniless, several hundred miles to a town where he was studying. The couple lived together and Joyce became pregnant. On the question of contraception, or lack of it, Luke is unusually clear and honest.

'As a man I continue to think along the lines – even now that I'm no longer an adolescent, as I was then – that if the woman is older than I am, then she can look after it herself. It is her responsibility as an adult, and I am something less than an adult. I have this covert attitude. It's irrational, now especially, but there is still that subconscious attitude that if the woman is older then it's her responsibility. It's wrong, but I certainly felt it very strongly as a seventeen year old.'

Luke has no idea how he obtained this attitude, which is balanced by the fact that he would assume contraceptive responsibility for a girl of his own age or younger. This ambivalence, he is sure, has nothing to do with the family's Catholicism. The children were not brought up with a slavish regard for Catholic dogma, and his mother has long practised contraception. Interestingly, Luke is adamant that he received no information about contraception from his parents, but his mother claims that both she and his father talked to him about it, particularly when he began to see a lot of Joyce. 'I begged him not to leave it to her.'

Obviously this breakdown in family communication can only be of technical interest before the fact of Joyce's pregnancy. How does a seventeen year old boy react to this situation?

'My senses were completely dulled. I did not really comprehend the whole implication of it. I suppose I began with a resolve to stand by my responsibilities, whatever they were and whatever the consequences. I had a sort of protective relationship and attitude towards Joyce. She was very insecure, always. On the rare occasions when she felt secure, she didn't need me at all. But, of course, with the pregnancy she seemed to need me desperately. So I felt I was fulfilling a useful role. I thought at that time I could help her. In fact, I thought, fancifully, that having a child would help her. I suppose by that time I did love her. Had I been able to regard the situation objectively, it would have appeared as hopeless as it appeared to everybody else.'

There was, of course, no question of marriage because Joyce was still a married woman. Had she not been, Luke thinks that they almost certainly would have married, 'and it would have been a folly'.

'The first thing we did was to try and get the child aborted. We went through the proper channels. She went into a nursing home and she was there for two days and she ran away twelve hours before the operation. She decided that she wasn't going to do it. She had a fit of resolve. I didn't have any such fit of resolve. I wasn't resolved enough. I wasn't persuasive enough. I wasn't sure enough of myself to say categorically that this was my decision on her behalf. I wanted her to have the child aborted. Maybe had I given this sort of support, she would have had the child aborted.'

When news of the pregnancy reached Luke's parents, through a mutual friend, they mounted quite a strong campaign in favour of adoption. Luke's mother was prepared to explore this solution on their behalf, and to foster the child prior to legal adoption. Because this idea originated with Luke's family, Joyce resisted it. Instead the couple started the preliminaries of adoption themselves. In fact, prospective adopters were found for Matthew before he was born and a foster home, not Luke's parents, was arranged. Joyce apparently accepted this but stipulated that she did not want to see the child. Three days after the birth, Joyce announced that a nurse had shown the baby to her and that she now wished to keep him. Still undecided, Luke argued that they should allow the baby to go to the foster home and that he and Joyce should use the six week interim period to consider all the implications of keeping their son. After only three weeks they collected the baby from the foster home, thus putting an end to the adoption proceedings.

Luke lost his place at the college and found great difficulty in getting any reasonably paid work as an unqualified eighteen year old. He, Joyce and the baby lived first in a shared student flat, and then in an inadequate bed-sitting room, with shared kitchen and bathroom facilities.

'I was always very much pleased to be a father and very sure of myself in dealing with the baby. Much more so than Joyce as a mother. I suppose that if one were to analyse it, it may have been that she resented being shown up to be a poor parent in the light of my being an adequate day-to-day parent, whereas she didn't like being a mother at all. She couldn't really work up a continuity of pride about the child. She couldn't sustain a successful maternal attitude. Sometimes she did everything and enjoyed it, and then she would lose all interest in the child. She would resent the fact that she couldn't function as she used to as a single woman.

'I think my main anxiety after he was born, my immediate reaction was, For God's sake don't let this happen again. Don't let any other babies happen in any situation, and I said, "Now you must get contraceptives." She said no, she didn't want to. So this immediately destroyed our sex life. I wasn't happy in bed thinking I might be procreating every time. She did eventually go to her doctor and got the pill, and the day she got it, she said, "Right, now I'm free. You'll have to watch out for yourself. I won't be sticking around here much longer."

As the relationship deteriorated, Luke's resolve shifted more and more towards his son. He no longer felt that he could help Joyce, but his commitment to the baby inevitably demanded that he accept her as well. They returned to stay with Joyce's relatives but were soon homeless again. While Joyce looked for a flat, Luke took Matthew to his parents and looked after him 'absolutely'. When a flat was found, some eight weeks later, the only sufficiently well paid work Luke could find entailed his going away again, to a seasonal job. He returned shortly before Matthew's first birthday and found that Joyce had become involved with another man whom she flatly refused to give up. At this point Luke walked out and, within two days, had left the country. 'I thought that I was really abandoning Matthew as I was abandoning her. I didn't think that I would have anything to do with him again.'

At her son's request, Luke's mother maintained contact with Joyce and the baby. What she saw made her aware of the very important service a sympathetic social worker can provide in such cases but Joyce 'resented any form of authority as Them, the enemy' and so no such help was forthcoming. This spotlights a dilemma, undoubtedly familiar to many social workers, that those most in need of help are often those who most resist it. The frightening thing is that had Luke's mother not been on hand, she feels that 'it might have become a very tragic situation'. Fortunately, after a few months, Joyce deposited the baby with Luke's mother who immediately began to explore the possibility of adoption once again. She informed Luke of the situation but he did not return at once 'because I thought this was just another temporary situation. I'd much rather not get involved once more with the child and become so attached to him again.'

Then came the idea, suggested to Luke's mother by a child-care officer with whom she had been in touch, that Luke should file an order with a magistrate requesting to be made legal guardian of his illegitimate son.

'Nobody had very much hope that I would succeed, really. My solicitor, even though he recognized the validity of my case and thought that I should, by rights, succeed, he didn't think that we had all that much chance. Obviously her solicitors thought the very same thing on her behalf; that she would win as the biological mother. I was, I think, so very lucky in so many ways. I had a very competent barrister, for a start, whereas Joyce's solicitor hadn't bothered to get a barrister's representation at all. There was also a very competent young probation officer who made the report. Joyce was on probation, which made her position more difficult. She hadn't bothered to get a job, she hadn't bothered to make a display of being ready to accept the child. She hadn't prepared a bedroom for him. She hadn't been saving up money. So she was in a bad position in court, which was my luck, and Matthew's luck, really. But in fact I got the impression from her appearance in court and from the whole presentation of her case that she didn't want to win. In her more coherent, lucid moments, she used to admit that she was not a good mother, that she would never be a good mother. It distressed her, having to look after a child, but she hadn't got the courage to renounce him. She had to have that important decision made for her, and the only people who could make it for her, ultimately, were the court. So I got absolute custody and there was no real difficulty.'

This idea of 'the objective good of the child' raises the whole question of privilege and social class which I believe to be important elements in this case and to the whole question of the involvement of unmarried fathers with their children.

Everything one learns about Joyce, her disturbed and unhappy background, her instability and periods of general social inadequacy, suggests that she would be ill-equipped to cope with the machinery of the law. It seems reasonable to suggest that her 'them-and-us' mentality, noted by Luke's mother, would extend to the law itself and, inevitably, to Luke and his family. Therefore, it is not unlikely that her failure to make any show of preparing a home and of providing support for Matthew stems either from a pernicious form of class paralysis when faced with 'them', or from a general fatalism born of a resentful recognition that the battle was unequal.

For example, it may be an adequate explanation for Joyce's solicitors' failure to retain a barrister to suggest that they did not consider it necessary but rather trusted in the traditional supremacy of the biological mother's claim, but it is also not impossible that this failure was again a symptom of fatalism, or even simple lack of money. One certainly hopes that Luke is right when he says that Joyce did not seem to want to win, and his remark about her needing to have this decision taken out of her hands undoubtedly fits the portrait one gains of her. But a positive lack of any will to win argues an objectivity about the personal disadvantages of having Matthew in her custody which does not seem likely of a woman in Joyce's state of mind.

Luke, on the other hand, had all the advantages of a secure, upper-middle class background and education. He is articulate, intelligent and in no sense in awe of the law or the social services. Above all, he could count on the moral and, even more important, the financial support of his parents. One must beware, therefore, of seeing the happy outcome of this particular case as an indication that men in general will increasingly assume this degree of responsibility for their illegitimate children. Quite apart from lacking most if not all of Luke's advantages, a working-class boy in a comparable situation probably would not even conceive of the idea of looking after his illegitimate child. In the first place the concept of 'the objective good of the child' is likely to be alien to him. Then, 'men don't look after children' and, in any case, the necessity of earning his own living would make the whole exercise virtually impossible. Again Luke's mother's observations are relevant.

'Had Luke not had our support, I suppose he would have been able to claim about £12·50 a week social security. It would have been very hard for a young man to make a good home, even an adequate home for his son on that. In fact, of course, he wouldn't have got custody and Matthew would have gone into care.'

In this case 'the objective good of the child' must have been an easy matter to resolve and this is, rightly, the prime consideration of the courts. However, a number of question marks hang over this point. The claim of the biological mother is still a very persuasive force to many, and it is easy to imagine that had Joyce shown herself to be only a little more capable, she might have won. Then again, had Matthew been a girl, one wonders if the court would have reached the same decision.

In many cases, of course, what the respective parents can offer the child is far less easy to define, in which case, given the existing expectations of society, and the respective position with regard to work etc. of men and women, it is entirely probable that only a few men, and then only ones who share the privileges of a Luke, will even apply for, let alone obtain custody of their illegitimate children.

It is very easy to regard legal proceedings of this nature in the abstract, yet they essentially concern people and their emotions. There was always a distinct and very clearly perceived possibility that Luke would not gain the custody of his son. Had this been so, how would he have felt? What would he have done?

'I would have followed up whatever appeals I could have made and had they failed I would simply have taken up my life where I left it off. My parents and I conferred about this and we decided that the only thing to do would be to abandon him completely. Not to present him with a small token of a father who visited him occasionally, or the short taste of a pleasant grandparents' house. I would in fact have gone abroad, and my parents would have ceased to communicate with Joyce. In the classic situation, where the putative father is estranged from the mother *and* the child, I would want to be available to this pair, were they in need of me, practically, from the point of view of money, security, but otherwise, no.

'Obviously I'm attached to Matthew, I always have been. I loved him from the day he was born. It was very hard for me to leave him when I did. It was a great strain for me to break away from him, but I'm sure that I would not have placed these emotional ties in front of the objective good of the child. I'm sure I wouldn't have done that. Had I been leaving him in safe hands, I would have left him. I'm not in any way dependent upon him, even now, for my mental security. I can survive without him. I know that. It wouldn't break me to leave him. No. It would be pretty terrible, but it would only be terrible from his point of view.'

Joyce was granted weekly access to Matthew by the court. She did not exercise this right immediately but once she did her visits quickly developed into trips out with Matthew and Luke, and then she demanded to be allowed to have her son alone with her. Luke, of course, agreed, but with some trepidation. He was, and is, afraid that Joyce will reveal her true relationship to Matthew.

'Obviously he must be told. I want it to be my decision, absolutely. I want to be in complete control of all this vital information being passed on to him. I want to choose precisely the right time, the right circumstances.'

In addition, he has no trust in Joyce's abilities to care for the child properly. He felt that he was spoiled and over-excited by these visits, which obviously put a strain on everybody. Underlying the very real fear of Joyce making a premature disclosure of her actual relationship to Matthew, one glimpses a fundamental conflict of attitudes to the way in which a child should be treated and brought up.

'She bought him a book. Sent it to him in the post. I brought it along one day and said, "Read it to him". She kept it by her side but she never bothered to read it to him. I thought this was strange. She had a box of his old toys which she gave to him and she appalled me by. . . He would build something with bricks and it was she, not him, who came along and knocked it down, with a shout and a scream. She was very raucous. There was no quietude and no introspection at all. She discouraged it and she was very bad with him in fact. So this was the thing that upset me most. The fact that made me want to move away from my parents' house, that made me want to do something else.'

Luke himself was in a far from ideal situation. Looking after Matthew made it almost impossible for him to find a job and he felt that he was vegetating, while his fears about Matthew's contact with Joyce disrupted his peace of mind. The opportunity to get away and to lead a more balanced life was provided by friends of his parents. Luke had known them all his life and has, in part, grown up with their children. They, however, have a late child, a little boy of three – the same age as Matthew when Luke agreed to talk to me. They also happen to live near an adult education college which operates during hours commensurate with the needs of single parent families and married women. Luke and Matthew stayed with this family and the two children became firm friends. Luke obtained a place at the college and it was while waiting for his grant that he invited the local social security office to think of him as an unmarried mother.

Before leaving, Luke informed Joyce of his plans, explaining that access would thus be difficult and necessarily irregular. Her reaction was to order both Luke and Matthew out of her home and she has not seen them since.

Luke now lives with this family, attends college and shares in the domestic routine necessitated by two small boys. He is grateful for this support, without which he says neither he nor Matthew could survive. This, he believes is the best life he can

C

provide for Matthew at the moment. He has a sibling figure and a grandmother who is 'mummy' without in any way pretending to be the child's mother. Luke remains the constant, stable figure in the child's life and he thinks this arrangement is preferable to the obvious alternative of allowing Matthew's grandparents to become substitute parents. The next step is to adopt his son himself. If he succeeds in this, he feels that he will have made the future as secure as is at present possible; security being the prime condition for Matthew learning the truth, eventually, about his parentage.

As we have seen, and as Luke himself recognizes, none of the really crucial decisions about Matthew's future could have been taken without the support of his family, his friends and especially his mother. This bears out the views of social workers who believe that involvement of the unmarried father, especially when these are very young men, depends upon their receiving the support of their parents. Too often, parents actually discourage their son's involvement in the situation, which is why I believe the participation of Luke's mother to be so important. It was in fact she who contacted me and outlined Luke's situation in a letter, explaining that Luke himself was far too busy to see, let alone to respond to my appeal for interviewees. This in itself was remarkable and Luke's subsequent willingness to talk to me testifies to the strength and harmony of their relationship. Although she has come to play a very important role *vis-à-vis* Matthew and Luke, she began from the standpoint of all mothers faced with this situation, being 'absolutely appalled and horrified' when she learned that Joyce was pregnant. Even if marriage had been a possibility, she would have opposed it. She always felt that 'the baby was more to pin down Luke than a mistake'. She was, in short, protective towards her son, to whom she had been very close and from whom she was then temporarily estranged without, probably, having any clear idea why. Certainly she saw Luke's life in ruins.

Implicit in everything that Luke and his mother say is a mutual dislike between Joyce and his mother. It is difficult to see how this could have been otherwise. From the family's point of view, Joyce must have represented a very real threat to Luke's future while their solidarity and 'interference' must have aggravated Joyce's general insecurity. They must have seemed formidable adversaries, especially to one for whom family support and stability was scarcely a commonplace.

Luke's mother showed her practical willingness to help from the very start, by offering to arrange adoption and to foster the baby for the initial period. Increasingly, however, Matthew's needs became a determining factor in her decision to assume more and more responsibility. Today, her main worry seems to be about maintaining the best role towards Matthew.

'I try to be the mother figure without pretending I am the mother. It is tricky because Matthew badly wants to attach to me and the natural reaction is to respond. But he isn't here with me for whole stretches of the time. What must he think? I mean a child in a normal family, wouldn't he find it terrible to be parted from his mother so much? This worries me a great deal, but as with the whole saga from the beginning I just play by ear and do what seems best as it arises. Luke follows much the same pattern as I set with my children. I leave decisions to him, but I try to soften his rather over-strict demands on Matthew. I think he tries to redress the balance of a lot of people being very kind and even sorry for Matthew.'

The experience of Luke's mother shows that instinctive reactions can be overcome and need not prevent parents exerting a positive and beneficial influence on the situation. Little as she would wish to be held up as an example, I believe that she and her family present one that could help other parents of unmarried fathers and mothers.

Much as one admires Luke's resolve to accept his responsibilities and build the best possible life for Matthew, one must also remember that, for such a person, facing up to the consequences of their actions is not a remote abstract duty, but provides an essential and entirely laudable emotional fulfilment. Quite simply, Luke seems to function best in a position of defined responsibility and, hindsight suggests, given the failure of his relationship with Joyce, the fact that he would take care of Matthew was almost inevitable. Even so, he is still only twenty-one. His life has taken a new direction as a result of these events and is greatly, though by no means insupportably, limited by Matthew's needs. Yet, in many ways, Luke's lot is a considerably easier one than that faced by most ummarried mothers.

'Social disapproval? No, I don't think so. From a feminist, a woman's liberationist point of view, this is rather depressing, that a man in this situation is accepted, is lauded and admired for his perseverance and his courage, whereas a woman is ostracized. I've never had any expression of disapproval about it since I've accepted my responsibility. Before then, yes. But in those days I was the putative father who had abandoned his child. Then I got the traditional disapproval. But since then, it's difficult to say. My fellow students, for instance, many of them are divorced or widowed or estranged from their husbands and they identify with my situation very easily. The fact that I don't happen to be married is completely irrelevant. I really don't know what the reaction is. I think it is simply that I am slightly intriguing and curious. Now since I was eleven I've enjoyed appearing to be curious and intriguing and an anomaly of some sort or another to my contemporaries. And with Matthew I've managed to retain this. I enjoy this singularization. I don't think otherwise that people's reaction to me is particularly relevant. I don't produce in people an automatic stereotyped reaction because people haven't come across this. They haven't got a stereotype for this situation, whereas for an unmarried mother there is a stereotyped reaction which everybody is aware of, but there's no such thing for me, no.'

Thus the traditional double standard which society is pleased to operate towards men and women is incorporated into new situations. How often is an unmarried mother lauded and admired for assuming her proper responsibility for her child? On the contrary, it sometimes seems that the best she can hope to receive is that acutely demoralizing reaction – pity. Nothing in society's attitude encourages her to make the best of her situation, to accept the limitations on her life that raising a child inevitably imposes. A woman, just as much as a man, may have to forego career opportunities, yet nobody admires her self-sacrifice, or helps to provide alternatives. No matter how one argues, a woman, by becoming an unmarried mother, no matter how responsibly she reacts to this situation, no matter how self-sacrificing she is, is lessened by her 'status'. Because we expect, without question, that women must bring up children, we do not praise her for doing so, but when a man does so, it becomes a matter for universal admiration and support. It is impossible not to conclude that just below the liberal social surface there lingers a strong belief that the problems faced by the responsible unmarried mother are just punishment for her having slept with a man before first assuring her own and her baby's future in wedlock.

Then again, being a man Luke is not expected to live alone with children, a fact which greatly depresses many of his female fellow students who are forced to do exactly that. It is generally assumed that he must have some external interests and he is able to find the practical help, albeit through the generosity of friends, to enable this. Such help is seldom readily forthcoming for the unmarried mother. The reaction which greets men like Luke is indeed heartening – not least because of the beneficial effect it must ultimately have on the child – but one's instinct to applaud must be qualified until the same reaction is automatically accorded to the unmarried mother.

The obvious solution to Luke's situation, as his doctor recently pointed out, is that he should marry. Luke accepts this, but also insists that it is not something he can contrive. His sense of his own identity and needs is too strongly developed for him to seek a step-mother for Matthew rather than a wife for himself. Somehow, I doubt that this will be a problem for, quite apart from his own charm and intelligence, the fact that he has accepted Matthew so wholeheartedly is likely to make him more rather than less attractive to women. Nevertheless, playing an active part in the day-to-day care of his son limits his social opportunities, and the whole experience has left him with an antipathy towards casual sex. He is naturally cautious about future relationships with women and Matthew's presence will undoubtedly continue to influence this attitude. It is to his credit that he impresses one strongly as a man unlikely to make any mistake when the opportunity to form such a relationship offers itself. In the meantime, Luke finds it almost impossible to define the difficulties of being a completely involved unmarried father.

'If I was in any way basically incapable, of course I would have terrible difficulties, but so far, touch wood, I have been pretty capable. I find it very easy to give him what I believe is a good fatherly relationship and one that compensates slightly for his not having a mother. I find it entirely natural and entirely enjoyable. A positive thing for me. The most pleasurable parts of my life are the week-ends, when I spend all my time with the kids. This is great.'

There is a sense of anti-climax in Luke's story which I understand as an accurate measure of the success of the venture. If he were a young widower, we would not look for drama and difficulties. It is only that his position is unusual and unfamiliar that we perhaps feel slightly let down now that his and Matthew's lives are on an even keel. Luke has shown that men can raise children in a stable atmosphere alone and, indeed, that it may be easier for them to do so because so many of the pressures which dog the unmarried mother do not apply to them. If there is a general hope to be derived from Luke's experience, I believe that it lies in the speed and efficiency with which he has been able to establish a good and, as far as circumstances allow, an ordinary life for his son.

Boris: An eternal spectre of hope

Boris is an artist, and a man of deep religious faith. His manner is gentle and considerate. The events and emotions he recounts, therefore, almost seem to have happened to another person altogether. Yet there are common themes, from childhood to the present day. As he talks a pattern begins to emerge. Religion and art, for example. And sex. His mother was Jewish, his father a Roman Catholic. The result of the pressures upon them was, he says, that they both became lapsed.

'I wandered into the Church and the Synagogue out of my own curiosity. I went to a school that was Church of England, so I got another side of it. I wasn't circumcized. I didn't have a Bar-Mitzvah, and I knew nothing at all about the Catechism. I was brought up believing in God and that there was a man called Jesus. Then it was really up to me. It was the best possible religious education.

'But the religious side of my upbringing filtered through art. My father is a fine water-colour artist and his involvement with me was. . . He failed in every other way, but he succeded totally in setting fire to my ambition to become an artist. And he did it relentlessly, too. He didn't force me, but he gave me all kinds of encouragement. You see, my father never worked, never held a regular job down, and nobody ever questioned where the boxes of paints came from.

'My parents were remarkably naïve. I have visions of them making love, and being quite naked in the house. Yet the things they didn't understand, like masturbation and my desiring girls, were anomalies really, compared with what they were doing themselves. I mean, my mother told me that children came from a pill. I don't think that my father ever dreamed that he should be in any respect responsible for teaching me that things like that went on.

'The only sexual education I ever got from an authoritative body was the Scout Master, who buggered me. And a singularly unpleasant experience it was! He said, "This is what men and women do when they are together. This is how babies are born. But since there aren't any girls here, I'll show you, if you're interested." I wasn't, but he showed me all the same.

'I told my parents this had happened, and they were completely and absolutely amazed. They had no idea that this kind of thing happened. I had to tell my mother, later in life, what queers were.

'They were very unhappily married, so that although they lived together, they weren't together in the real sense. There was screaming, shouting, violence. Yes, I did mind it, terribly. It meant that, for a long period, from the age of about eleven to thirteen, I don't think I ever slept all night. I remember thinking that they would want to kill me. I mean, the corollary of them screaming and shouting was that I built up a phobia about them trying to poison me, or kill me, or allow me to die in some kind of way. It's odd that I drew that conclusion, but at the time it was the only tangible thing I could see.

'The only figure of authority in my life was my mother, and she loved me to such an extent that it was not wrong for me to do anything. Everything, but absolutely everything was totally permissible and, in fact, the more pain I caused her, the more, in a sense, she was fulfilled. I was the dominant person. I became a son and husband, really. She believed everything I said, implicitly, from the day I was born. She depended on me completely for every male task. I'm conscious of my femininity, really, having spent so much time with her.'

School was not a secure place, either. Boris's memories of that time revolve around art and sex, apart from a keen sense of gratitude to an art master who befriended and encouraged him.

'The fact that I had Jewish blood made me feel the burden of, and be the object of all misdemeanours that took place in the school. So I was punished quite regularly for things I'd not done, and beaten up just for being not like them. I was not anti-social. I didn't smash things up. I stole, but not terribly. My "delinquency" always took a sexual outlet. Always.

'I developed a sexual drive when I was five and always found either a member of my own sex, or of the other sex to indulge in sexual activities with me. I can remember my first desiring a girl, and having her, within the confines of a five year old's abilities. When authority of some kind or another, in those times, threatened me, it heightened the need for a sexual experience.

'All sexual acts, up to the age of fourteen, were done as a collective activity. It was part of being part of the gang, and finding some way to be accepted. I always mixed with older boys who liked me for my daring, because I would do things that they often themselves wouldn't do. It was the only way I could prove myself to them. You see, I was desperately unaccepted – unacceptable. It fired me to further depths of courage, by trying and getting girls into situations where they would respond to sexual activity, within groups. It seldom, if ever, took place outside a group, and, I might add, they hated me almost as much as the boys did. I was a very ugly child in terms of the Celtic-Christian appearance. My nose went the wrong way, and so on. And I could do things they couldn't do, like paint.

'Intercourse proper was almost impossible. It was such an excitement you could never quite get that far. The whole thing would be involved in other areas of sex. If it did happen, one was almost unaware that it was happening. I lived in complete ignorance. I had regular sexual relationships with girls through-out my adolescence, and still had no understanding of what I was doing. Although I had seen my mother and father having intercourse, I, for some reason or another, thought that you had intercourse standing up or lying on your side. Someone told me, purely by chance, how they had grazed their knees having a fuck on some concrete, and I deduced from what he told me that he had been kneeling down. I was fifteen or sixteen, which is for most people very young, but, as I say, I had an extraordinary sexual appetite. Throughout my teens I was ever-active, but it never occurred to me to lie on top of a woman to make love. So that shows the discrepancy between my personal desires and what I was told. In my case, it was standing up, or on my side in bombed-out buildings. It's not very comfortable. But it fulfilled me. I was happy as a result of having done that, and that was all that mattered at the time.'

Armed only with this mixture of sexual precocity and ignorance, Boris entered the junior department of an art school when he was fourteen. This, necessarily, must have set him further apart from his childhood peer-group. It may have increased the pressures on him. Inevitably, his adolescence continued within the art school situation, where he increasingly found himself falling romantically in love with remote and unobtainable girls. Eventually he formed a relationship with a girl and probably became an unmarried father for the first time. The obvious conclusion to draw, given the circumstances of Boris's childhood and background, is that such a situation was bound to arise.

This sort of background, however, does not share the middle-class embarrassment and silence about contraception. Boris remembers that the brand names 'Durex' and 'Ona' were an accepted and comprehended part of the language of the gang. Condoms floating in the river were a common sight, and sparked off speculative conversations. Consequently, when he did have a continuing sexual relationship with a girl, he was by no means ignorant of a contraceptive method, but he did not employ it. His attitude is a familiar, if rather vague one, and it sorts oddly with the increasing responsibility he felt for this and subsequent women.

'Well, you know, I would come inside when she said she was safe. I've never really been able to work that out, either. I've just taken their word for it. Someone told me you needed thermometers. . . That's maths and I'm no good at that, so I've always trusted them.'

'I suddenly became very desirable, for some reason or another that I have never understood. I think I must have been about nineteen when I fell in love with someone who loved me as deeply. That lasted for about a year, and in very tragic circumstances, heightened by the fact that I had TB, and was dying. I went away to try to cure myself. She became pregnant and the whole affair ended in absolute and utter disaster. Her mother whisked her off to a mental home. I never knew where it was. She had told me that her periods had stopped, but she attributed that to the fact that she was losing weight more rapidly than I was. Anyway, her mother wrote to me saying I must never get in touch with her again. She wouldn't tell me where she was. I drove around various places, trying to find her and I couldn't. The outcome of that pregnancy will never be clear because I've never seen her since and I don't know what's happened to her.

'We thought, I think, that it wouldn't matter. I think we wanted to get married, and we wanted to be with each other forever. The notion of a child had not impinged on our consciousness at all. To me, the notion of getting a job and going to work was utterly remote. My desires in life were wholly towards gratification through her, and working, and getting pissed. . . So a child was behind a series of many walls.

'I've never seen pregnancy as being an abstract concept. It's always been in terms of there being a child, partly because I think I've never entertained the notion of abortion, although there have been dozens as a result of me.'

Even in this first relationship the fact that he felt himself to be loved *as* deeply as he loved is significant. Just as he had discovered a sense of identity within the gang through his sexual exploits, so in this private relationship his identity had to be confirmed through love. Boris's insecurity, and the subsequent measures he took to combat it, were greatly influenced by having had this girl literally taken away from him.

From this point on in his story, Boris's desire to be loved for himself and not as an ideal in some woman's head is increasingly expressed. This should not be mistaken for arrogance, since Boris's career developed rapidly. He became successful and, for a short time, was something of a public figure. During that period the number of pregnancies he caused were 'legion, and they all ran very much to a pattern'. Most of the women were married and none put any sort of pressure on him. The woman concerned had a tendency to move away, or to be entirely equivocal about his paternity. This he describes as 'ironical and somehow indicative of the whole mess of that side of my life'. One thing is certain, Boris was very attractive to women, partly, one suspects, because of his *cachet*, and partly because of his obvious vulnerability. He tended to prefer women older than himself, or much younger, and no doubt this had a great deal to do with his early acceptance of the dual role of son and husband to his mother. He also points out, with a noticeable irony, that 'the artist is an eternal spectre of hope' to women.

Boris may never have entertained the notion of abortion, but he was forced to do so in the next significant relationship he formed.

'She became pregnant through her own fault. She wanted to be pregnant and then, when she actually became pregnant, she was frightened to go through with it. Against all my pleadings, she had abortions on both occasions. She threatened suicide and I had to capitulate. It destroyed the relationship. I don't think it was guilt. The most important thing, it showed that we really weren't compatible in that sense. What it did was, it heightened her emotional view of the world, and it decreased my own emotional view of the world. We started to grow apart because we started to view the world in different ways. She accused me, but I didn't accept the guilt, because I didn't feel I was really guilty. I wanted to marry her and settle down and have the kid, but she was just frightened of her mother. It wasn't the guilt that destroyed the relationship. So much was the horror of the idea of having a child that when she really wanted one, and to settle down and marry me, I wanted nothing but to get away.

'That was a trauma I've never really got over. I feel and think more about that few months in my life now than I've ever done in the past. At the time, it was too terrible to contemplate. I'm against abortion and have been in the cases of all the women I've known because I haven't known one woman who's had an abortion and who's the better for it, a better woman for it, and a happier woman for it.'

Boris is here expressing two familiar masculine attitudes. That it is the girl's fault that she becomes pregnant, and that abortion is a thoroughly bad thing. It is not perhaps too fanciful to see here a wish to abrogate responsibility in an untenable situation and a wish not to have the identity-confirming child destroyed. Many men do experience a sense of personal identity through paternity and, as becomes increasingly clear, this was certainly important to Boris, although he was obviously not conscious of it at the time.

During the death-throes of this relationship, another began. In the telling, Boris elected to call the women concerned Miss A and Miss B. They, together with Boris and others, begin to sound like characters in a French farce, except that the action is never funny.

'When I decided that Miss A and I could no longer carry on living together, that we were destroying each other completely, I met Miss B. It was love at first sight. I mean, I was looking for anything or anyone who could relieve me from my burden of a woman I had once loved deeply and now hated – such were the pressures put on me to now marry her and settle down and have children. I wanted these things, but I didn't want them from her. I could only see a life of misery ahead.

'Miss B was of a mixed nationality, with all the succulent drippings of the Russian/French mixture, with a bit of Hungarian thrown in. The full vibrance of the body was a joy to behold. Men fell over themselves to do what they could for her. She was, in every way, a vulnerable person, I think. She had traversed the earth with this tiny child, who was a very beautiful version of herself with blonde hair. Something in me evoked something in her and it was love at first sight. We had an absolutely wonderful, terrible, ill sick kind of relationship, yet she was the one for me. I was absolutely and utterly captivated in a way I had never been before.

'There was still Miss A and she had to be dealt with. She tried to kill herself, and the final catharsis of our relationship was so bloody that the bleakest hours of my life were spent on the night she tried to kill herself. The long and the short of it is that Miss A was finally secured into a niche of unhappiness, but away from the suicide situation, and Miss B came here.

'Now Miss B's mother lives in France and, on the same night that Miss A tried to commit suicide, Miss B's mother tried to commit suicide. So she had to fly back with the child. I played a waiting game here, and Miss B said that she had to go with her mother to Yugoslavia, to recuperate. Letters of her adoration and superhuman love poured in through the box every day.

'Well, then they suddenly stopped, you see, and I went off to

Yugoslavia, thinking the worst had happened. I went all the way to the hotel and found that she had disappeared. I came back to London in the most terrible state. There was one woman in hospital, and the other woman gone.

'Finally, she arrived back, and I telephoned her in France. She said, "I've got something to tell you. I've been unfaithful." At that point I couldn't take any more. I couldn't believe it. I went to France and did everything possible to win her back again because I had put all my money on her. I had staked my life on her.

'Anyway, we reached a compromise, one I was never really convinced by. We agreed that she should sell all the things in France, and she would come and live here, and we would get married. This took place in the August and the whole thing went on until about three days before Christmas. By then, of course, I had completely eaten myself up, and was demanding that she came here, because every time she said she was coming, some other thing would prevent her.

'Finally she came, not with her child, as I had expected, but with her brother who was wanted by the police. So I had to find somewhere for him, and she was here, and then Miss A wanted to kill herself again and we had her on the phone all the time. And in between all this, we had a fuck. And as a result of this, a pregnancy occurred.

'She went back at Christmas, saying goodbye, and I was really glad to see her go. I thought, at least, that's over. In the middle of January – I was now by no means interested in her coming back – the phone rang and it was her saying she was pregnant and I was the father. I asked her what she was going to do, and she said, "Well, of course, I'll come now." I didn't have the courage to say, "I don't want you to come."

'So she came, with two truck loads of furniture, her little girl and her mother came, too. The three of them lived in my flat, with me in the front room, going slightly mad. She became gradually more and more pregnant. And no love from me, and no love from her to me. I was expedient to the whole situation. I had become the Jewish father-figure who fucks off in the morning and gets the money, and then they all spend it.

'I moved out and went to live with my present wife. She had a tiny room and had loved me, unknown to me, throughout these three years. When I needed a friend, there she was, and listened, and loved me, and took me in, and was gentle. So I went and stayed there, but I didn't tell them.

'So I was living there and, unbeknown to my wife, managed to occupy the beds of several other ladies, too, which was all very exhausting. But, of course, it was the kind of classic situation for me, being threatened on every level, being told that I must do this, I must marry Miss B, and, of course, I mustn't, didn't, wouldn't, couldn't. I just found that I had to have other women as outlets, and it was really the whole situation of my life completely enacted. The finale, really, of the whole period.

'One of the relationships that I struck up was with a girl who lived up the road. She was divorced, like Miss B, with a small child. And I made her pregnant, too, and she was going into hospital six weeks after this one. Thank God, I say thank God, she had a miscarriage.

'It was a nightmare. I had to keep them all from each other; make clandestine telephone conversations. I did my work in some woman's bedroom. I did my living and eating with my present wife. I came back here to pick up materials, and actually, I think I went to the woman up the road for sheer animal lust. Just to see if I existed still. And I had a friend whose marriage was breaking up, and he left his wife three weeks before a baby was due. I was having to go to her in the afternoons to stop her doing all sorts of injuries to herself. And she was saying I'd have to marry her, too. Everyone was saying I had to marry them.

'I told Miss B that I didn't love her and that she must go back to France. In all this the man she had run off with in Yugoslavia turned up. Then a flatmate from France turned up, with her husband, and he said that Miss B had told his wife that she wasn't sure that the baby was mine. So I went into a cold sweat, because I really felt I had been gipped all along the line. Everything she had promised, she had broken. Everything she told me had proven to be a lie, and this was the last straw, really.

'So I confronted her with this and asked her if it was true. "Oh, how can you when I am pregnant?" She had hysterics. Her mother came in. I was a *monstre,* and this awful woman would throw things at me. I was thrown out, physically ejected, and so I never really knew the truth of all that.

'When it was ultimately born, we searched for clues and found many that we thought might relate I and it. In the end, I thought, Well, it's a fair cop, guv. You've not paid for any of the others. It could be yours. So off they toddled, two years ago, mother, baby, daughter and all, and that was the last I saw of them. I pay her three quid a week.'

'Yes, the baby was born in England. Yes, I did see it. It was a little boy . . . girl. No, I think nothing about the child, nothing at all. I'd resent paying if it wasn't mine. I'd resent having had to go through it all if I was just being used. I resent it to a certain extent, but I would resent it completely. . . Ultimately I wouldn't resent it, because I don't view the world in that way.'

Since this frenetic finale, many things have changed for Boris. He is happily and devotedly married, and the emergence of his faith is obviously connected with his having had to put his emotional house in order.

'I've learned forgiveness as a result. In all these situations, I have been forgiven by the people. Each one of them has forgiven me, and I have understood what forgiveness is.'

Because of this, he can be unusually objective about himself. For one thing, he accepts that he tried to make both Miss A and Miss B pregnant, in order to secure the relationship. In the the case of Miss B, the pregnancy occurred too late, when he least wanted it, but in the early stages of their relationship he intuitively saw the possibility of a child as a device with which to bind her to him.

This is, of course, commonly the way women are supposed to behave. It spotlights in Boris not so much that strong animal of which, as an artist, he is deeply conscious, nor that essentially practical 'femininity' which he attributes to his childhood relationship with his mother, but his unusual emotional dependence on women. In each of these relationships, the need to be confirmed, through love, as an individual is apparent, but it is complicated by several factors. Having been the centre of his mother's universe, he thinks that it would have required something very dramatic indeed to prevent him seeking comparable relationships elsewhere. Equally important is the fact that it is only comparatively recently that he has been able to see himself as a genuinely creative artist. Throughout the period described, he was preoccupied with commercial art, and he acknowledges with affection that Miss A was intuitively aware that he needed to concentrate on his own work. Although Boris now has a strong sense of identity, as an artist and a husband, he still maintains:

'It is true now that if I'm threatened, the first thing I do is look for a woman, or become sexually aroused in some way. And it's quite incidental to painting. I mean, painting exists all the time, and there isn't a moment when I wouldn't be wanting to work. But then why should it be related, anyway, except that I get more sexually stimulated when I'm working? Besides, sexual passions don't frighten me like they used to.'

Boris's attitude to women is that of a cherisher. He would like to buy all his wife's clothes, if she would let him. If he had the time, he would like to do all the housework and cooking. She must want for nothing. Of his mother now, he says:

'I'm just very sorry that she never learned to develop herself other than through me. Yet I know that I could never have done anything unless she made the sacrifices that she did. I just feel a bit sorry that she didn't spend a bit more, at the time she was able to, on herself.'

It seems that any woman he loves has to be repaid for this sacrifice, and because 'it would be true to say that all the women have been a solace': a sort of emotional blanket he pulled over himself to escape the threat of authority.

There is no such person as the typical unmarried father, but in two respects at least, Boris illustrates what appear to be common elements in the make-up of the species. Firstly, the broken and disturbed home, in his case aggravated by the school and social situation, which creates a need to be loved, by hook or by crook. Any lengths, even an unwanted child, are justifiable in so far as they provide the emotional security and the confirmation of identity which is so desperately sought. The reality of the child plays very little part in this, it seems, but the prospect of fathering a child is a common means of proving one's identity.

Secondly, there is the whole question of contraception. Boris maintains that when he inadvertently made Miss B pregnant – and at that time he was emotionally exhausted and genuinely wanted to be free of her – that was the only occasion on which *coitus interruptus* failed to be an effective means of contraception. So firmly does he believe this that he attributes his occasional doubts about his actual paternity primarily to the unlikelihood of failure with this 'method'. Experts, on the other hand, are entirely agreed that so unreliable is this technique that it is unworthy to be considered as a means of contraception at all. Yet, from a very early age, Boris was conversant with the nature and use of condoms. Like hundreds, perhaps thousands of other men, he never seriously considered using them. Whether this is because they do directly interfere with the pleasure of the act, or because men are, on the whole, essentially unaware of what an unwanted pregnancy actually means, is arguable. In Boris's case at least it would seem that the strong element of risk involved in *coitus interruptus* was linked with his identity problems and with the wish to bind his partner to him through pregnancy. As a footnote, it is perhaps worth recording that, although neither his wife nor Boris wish to have children yet, he accepts that she will want them and that they will have them. Meanwhile, 'She's on the pill, now, much against my will.'

Andrew: Unmarried daddy

'It's been three periods, really. First of all, when I met Janet, I felt nothing about her. Then I really grew to Janet. I mean when that baby was born. . . Apparently, the father's just interested in how the mother is and the mother's just interested in how the baby is. Well, that was certainly just so with me. When the baby came along, I knew and was there, I knew it existed and I knew it was all right and was a girl, but all I could do was put my arms around Janet and give her a kiss and say, "Thank you. I'm really happy that you've given me a little baby. You've fulfilled me, in a way, as a man, as well as yourself as a woman." It was a terribly close experience. The climax, as it were, of really feeling for her was when the kid was born.

'I'm getting bored. If it weren't for the kid, well, possibly things wouldn't stay together for very long. The child has been my own peace of mind, my own contentment. That the child is content, smiles. . . It recognizes me, its father, but now Janet has become pretty bossy, which is totally alien to me because, rightly or wrongly, I've got this thing that a woman shouldn't boss a man. If there's anything that gets my goat it's that. And she's getting more and more bossy; telling me what to do with my kid; telling me what to do with that, and telling me what to do with something else. So I'm sort of getting bored and looking for a way out of the situation. I mean, I still have some feeling, quite a lot of feeling, really, there for her, but she's pretty rigid, I'm afraid, and rather narrow in her outlook.'

Andrew is twenty-six, a student about to re-sit the finals he ploughed the year before because of the stresses and strains of Janet's pregnancy. Janet, five years younger, is also a student and they met in a hostel where both were then living.

'This was a year last November and, as luck would have it, I must have made Janet pregnant the very first night I slept with her, because in fact I didn't sleep with her after that for a good two or three months because I was going out with someone else at the same time. I've had many casual relationships and this was just another one as far as I am concerned. When I go to bed with a woman I don't tend to say, "Well, right, I'd like to go out with you for the next five months", or whatever. I am just out to enjoy myself.

'I may have slept with Janet, yeah, once or twice, immediately before I went home for Christmas. I thought, over Christmas, that Janet wasn't the girl for me, and when I come back I'll finish with her, because I was getting bored, quite honestly. I came back to find that she was pregnant. She came to see me. It was a Friday evening. She was upset. She hadn't told anyone else. So she was all screwed up inside, and she just sort of stammered out, "Andrew, I'm pregnant." I was obviously immediately in a bit of a fix, wondering what to do. I felt very guilty, and a rotten bastard really, because the girl, in her own way, is a nice girl.

'Before, if anything like this would have happened, I'd have said, "Right, woman, straight out of the door. I don't want to know anything about it. Forget it." But because this particular girl really was very innocent... She'd absolutely no one to stand on, or stand by her apart from me.'

Janet's parents died while she was a child. She and her elder sister were brought up by legal guardians and educated in boarding schools. She felt, at first, unable to tell anyone, other than Andrew, of her condition. When, later, she did inform her guardians, they were less than helpful. Janet's inevitable dependence on Andrew, aggravated by her comparative inexperience and youth, certainly influenced his decision to stand by her. First he persuaded her to have a pregnancy test and, when this proved to be positive, 'I thought, well, Christ, what do I do? In a way I do want to get rid of the kid because I don't want this round my neck. I suddenly realized, you know. . . the impact hit me.' The hospital at which the test was made referred Janet to an obstetrician and Andrew accompanied her to the interview. Janet was offered an abortion but, because she was already three months pregnant, it was explained to her that this made an operation necessary. 'And, you know, my stomach sort of turned right over. I thought, Christ, you know, why should she suffer like this? Because, as I say, I was being a bastard. I was just using the girl really. And so the guilt then came back onto me.'

They were given a week in which to decide for or against the abortion.

'She was in favour of the abortion, but because of what it entailed, and the fact that they were going to start chopping her up – I just didn't want anyone to touch her. I tried to talk her out of it, but hoping that she would take the initiative. I mean, I wanted a decision from her that she wanted not to have the abortion, as opposed to me having to force her into it, or talk her into it.'

At first Janet concurred, but within a few days had changed her mind again in favour of abortion. 'That really made me feel a hell of a lot worse.' Andrew countered by pointing out the possible risks involved: the fact that she might become sterile, even that she might not recover from the operation, 'I was sowing everthing I could, really, to try and make her say, "I won't have the operation." '

The less radical alternative, marriage, does not ever appear to have been seriously considered, presumably because of Andrew's conviction that Janet was not the right girl for him.

'I don't think the fact of marriage. . . I mean, we both agree. Well, we've made two mistakes at the moment, don't let's make any more. Plus the fact that I don't think marriage would have entered into it anyway. We just had too much on. From what I've seen of married couples and what I've seen of life, I think that would certainly be totally the wrong way of going about it – to suddenly rush off and get married. That would have been the silliest thing we could ever have done. Marriage may have entered her mind. It may be entering it now but. . . I'm not against marriage and I'm not against marrying the right woman, but I don't think, quite honestly, that Janet's the right woman for me.'

Marriage having been ruled out, many men would have welcomed abortion as a solution to the problem, particularly as the girl herself was willing. Andrew, however, was determined to dissuade Janet from the operation. He was genuinely afraid of medical complications and unwilling to compound the guilt he already felt at having used her. But, probably with the rationalizing benefit of hindsight, he advances another reason.

'You see, essentially Janet had nobody in life, and one of the arguments against abortion was the fact that it would fulfil her life in more ways than one. It would give her something on which she could shower love as opposed to hiding herself away from society and people. Because she had nobody, apart from one sister. She's got something to love and give for now, something to live for whereas before her life was so drab. I mean, photographs of her before she met me, you could see that she was so desperately unhappy looking.'

If this statement is something more than a justification after the event, then it was an extraordinary decision to make for some one – for that is essentially what Andrew did – and particularly at that stage in the situation.

There may be a third factor which helped to bring about Andrew's one-man anti-abortion lobby. His mother is an orthodox Catholic and he was brought up in that faith, albeit in the teeth of his Communist father's considerable opposition. Now Andrew describes himself as a Catholic, 'but not in the way the church would like me to be. I used to be head altar boy and it was very nice, actually. I used to love singing and shouting around in Latin, until it changed to English. I only got something out of going to Church by being altar boy and saying things in Latin and doing all the little rituals, which I really enjoyed. But as for sitting out in the audience, sort of stuff, and having to listen. . . I began to realize that the church wasn't so infallible.'

Working on the principle that no born Catholic ever quite succeeds in shaking off the lessons learned in those crucial, formative years, it seems not unlikely that the Church's pronouncement against abortion influenced him, if only subconsciously. This is born out, I think, by his constant reference to the fact that the foetus was, at three months, 'fully formed', and he sometimes seems to imply that his objection would have been less strong had Janet's pregnancy not been so far advanced.

Fear for Janet, guilt because of Janet, his belief that a baby would fulfil her and give purpose to her life, and a possible lingering adherence to the established Catholic position on abortion probably all combined to make Andrew so determined to veto the abortion through Janet. Certainly, by this stage, he was already assuming dominant control of the situation, and of Janet.

At the time of the second hospital visit, Janet was still in favour of the abortion.

'She got very upset. And the doctor asked me what I thought and I said, "Well, I'm against abortion unless it's absolutely necessary. I realize what I've done and I don't particularly want Janet cut up." And he asked me if I would support the kid, what my feelings were. And I said, "Well, you know. I'm prepared to support the child. You know, it's my child. I don't care what difficulties come along, I'll face up to them. There's no reason why I shouldn't solve any problem that's put in front of me, really." '

They were given a few more hours in which to discuss the matter and decide.

'I was really again desperately trying to convince Janet, although not trying to force her, because obviously if I was pushing her then I wouldn't be satisfied for the rest of my life. I had to have her "yes", as it were, that she wouldn't have the abortion. I may have just eased her on the road to not having the abortion and she sort of struggled along it, as it were.'

In this way the first major decision was made, but it brought little relief.

'Although I'd made up my mind to face up to my responsibilities, I could see that in doing so I was putting a rope around my neck. But I couldn't see any other way out of it. I was just tearing myself apart, really.'

They now faced a series of practical problems which were often complicated and interrupted by medical and emotional crises.

It was clearly a case of one damn thing after another. First there was the question of Janet's grant and obtaining permission for her to complete her course after her confinement. In this, as in everything else, Andrew played the leading role. 'I took on an extremely protective feeling as soon as Janet was pregnant. Especially as I could see her growing bigger and bigger and bigger.'

Naturally, Janet did not wish to continue living in the hostel in her condition and the warden was by no means anxious to have her stay. Temporary accommodation was found for her in a Catholic Chaplaincy. By extending the period of his final examinations, Andrew narrowly avoided being asked to leave at once and thus managed to keep a roof over his own head, at least temporarily.

Like hundreds of other couples in this situation, they quickly discovered that accommodation for unmarried pregnant women is extremely difficult to find. The one place they did manage to see Andrew rejected as being too depressing for Janet. A social worker at the hospital eventually found a vacancy in a house run specially for unmarried mothers and it was arranged that Janet should go there after the birth of her baby. At the same time, Andrew was frantically trying to inform himself about available social services etc.

'I immediately looked up every single body I could think of, and went anywhere I could to get as much information about social services. Anything. No matter how remote. I'd ring them up and put the problem to them and ask did they have any advice? Yes, we went to a social worker. God, we took one look at the place and it was depressing. I felt really sorry for the girls who had no support, or had really bad circumstances because the place was dirty. We both got a very depressing outlook on the whole situation.'

Andrew even accompanied Janet to the ante-natal clinic where he learned something about the techniques of psychoprophylaxis.

'I went along for interest, plus the fact that Janet was also likely to forget, while she was actually giving birth, any particular process. I wanted to sort out, in fact, especially for me, what happens if we're caught, regardless of the ambulance service, and that kid comes along and I can't get an ambulance in time.

What do I do? I was looking at everything from Janet's point of view.'

Andrew's protectiveness towards Janet reached a sort of climax when, as a result of making love, he thinks, she began to haemorrhage and was rushed to hospital. Andrew refused to leave her side and this caused a series of aggressive encounters with the hospital staff.

'As far as I'm concerned, fine, they looked after her body, but I'm going to look after what's between the ears, which is just as important. So every spare minute of time I went in there. Again, less study for my exams, which by now I'd virtually given up hope of anyway. Unless miracles happened. I'm not that intelligent.'

With Janet released from hospital and the doomed exams failed, Andrew took a three week job in a factory, praying that the baby would not be born until the job was finished since he needed the money to finance his return to college. Again, no detail was neglected. He informed his employers that he might receive an urgent call from the hospital and obtained from them a telephone number at which he could be reached. Immediately, he had Janet test the effectiveness of this emergency system and, satisfied that it would indeed work, he got on with his job and the three weeks passed uneventfully. Janet went into labour the very night that his employment finished and their daughter was born.

'It was such an emotional relief for me. I just put my arms around her, kissed her and said, "Thanks, Janet. I'm really pleased with what you've done. You've given me a child."'

In spite of the fact that a home had been arranged for Janet and the baby some time before the birth, Andrew says that adoption was still a possibility.

'Again this was a very large thorn in my side. What am I going through this for if she's just going simply to give the kid away like that? I don't want to give my kid away. I said, "Look, Janet, if you don't want the kid, then fine. I want it. And if you're going to have it adopted then I'll really fight you in court for the custody of that child. I don't believe in just giving my kid away like that. It's just too important. It means too much to me, apart from what we've both gone through." She was in two minds about it. I thought I'd better have a look into adoption laws. Say, you know, "Well, regardless of what you want, Janet, I'm afraid the law has it that you've got to keep the kid for six weeks." Not true, of course, but I just didn't tell her the whole truth. She can foster it out for six weeks. This did arise later on and I said, "Well yes, Janet, you can foster it out if you wish." But I said, "What on earth are you going to do with all your milk? The thing is, you've never tried."

'I think that's the worst part about anything in life. If you never try, you've only yourself to blame. But if you do try, as hard as possible, and you fail, well, at least you've tried.

'I said, "Look, Janet, it's the same with babies. Give it a try. See what you think by holding it. You won't know anything about the baby unless you're going to hold it. If you haven't tried to do or feel something for that child, then you're going to feel it for the rest of your life. And so will I."

'I don't want to let anything go through life that's going to affect me later on, that would have serious consequences when I know that it is my own fault. In a way adoption would have been an easy way out. It might have been. But again, in the back of my mind there's this thing about not wanting to let go. It was a pattern of not wanting to let go. It runs throughout.

'I'd been encouraging my own feelings in Janet, in a way, by saying "Don't have the abortion. Keep the kid. Don't have the adoption." I'd been the guide-rail as such, which she keeps banging against. Although I've tried not to twist her arm behind her back. I was just hoping that she'd go along the right road and I'd keep nudging her every so often to make sure she'd stay on it.'

Inevitably, Janet agreed to keep the baby.

Throughout this difficult period, Andrew had no practical support himself. As a result of failing his finals, he had no grant and so was unable to contribute to the baby's upkeep in any significant financial way. Only in a moment of extreme stress did he confide in a few friends. His parents he did not tell until most of the major problems had been solved. Yet in many ways he derives strength from his family and it seems likely that many of his attitudes do stem from his background.

He is the eldest of seven children with, as already mentioned, a Catholic upbringing. They are a close family, displaying solidarity in the face of problems. His attitude towards women, protective yet superior, selfish yet concerned, is typical of many working-class men. His ambition, which he admits is fierce, is fed by having seen his father work extremely hard to raise a large family and also from his own educational difficulties. At fifteen he had to fight to stay at school. He now understands his father's point of view that he should have been earning and 'pulling his weight', but he was determined to remain at school. To do this he had, to a certain extent, to take the law into his own hands, both at home and at school. In this sense he has had to fight to get an education which explains why he is still determined, despite all the difficulties and lack of support, to re-sit his finals.

This background and the attitudes it has fostered is in direct opposition to Janet's and is an increasing source of disagreement between them. As the eldest of a large family, he is used to children in a way that Janet is not. 'Janet obviously had no idea how to hold the baby and I had to show her, and and how to change it and what have you.' He can count on his family's emotional support – his mother offers advice in her letters and longs to see her grandchild – while Janet's guardians have rejected her out of hand. Because her background has been very protected, Andrew derives considerable authority from his greater experience. Somewhere in the back of his mind there is the knowledge that his parents would accept his illegitimate daughter, although he has made no efforts to obtain custody of her. This must enable him to say, however, 'Looking at it from the kid's point of view, I think I could be both mother and father to it, give it its necessary love and feeling, warmth and security, just as much as any female.' Yet this possibility remains essentially unformulated and undetermined. The knowledge of family support and his own independent confidence lent him authority in argument. Janet, lacking any such support, is therefore in a less advantageous position, aggravated by her youth.

Having decided to keep the baby, the financial problem loomed large. Andrew returned to college without a grant and was hoping to be financed by charitable organizations. Janet had to obtain social security.

'O.K. Next comes social security, you see? My name's on the birth certificate. That's number one. Number two, they start to say, "Where's daddy?" You see? And, of course, not meaning to have Janet insulted as lots of poor, unfortunate girls are, going to social security, I said, "Well, how'd it be if somebody went down with you, so's you've got a witness of anything that's said?"

Anyway, we tried to work out some sort of story from the advice we'd been given from people who knew social security in this context. "Look, Janet, say you don't remember anything about it. You went to a party and met one, maybe two different men. Or, that you've had so many different men you don't know which man it is." Which is a bit degrading, really, and a bit disgusting, I think, from the point of view of social security, but I knew that we'd have to sort out social security and I'd have to support her, mentally, through this period.'

With the aid of a social worker this problem was solved and is, in any case, partially off-set by the fact that Janet has a little money of her own. She too has now returned to her studies and is living in the accommodation found for her earlier. The pressures, to an extent, are off. Andrew visits her and the baby several times a week, but many question marks still hang over the future.

'I would like my child to know me as her father. I want to support my kid throughout life. If she's in any crisis, I want to be there. If you've no one to turn to, that's when things are going to start to crumble. I want a good life for my child.'

For an unmarried father such wishes are invariably unrealistic. When, as in this case, a couple do not even live together and at least one of them is convinced that marriage would be a disaster, it is impossible for a man to realize his paternal desires without placing the girl in some sort of social limbo. Inevitably it has been pointed out to Andrew that Janet may want to marry and that in that event he will have to make some far-reaching decisions.

'If Janet does get married should I really consider whether or not it will be best to keep on as that girl's father? Now at the moment I couldn't consider leaving the baby. You see, if we do split up, one rule that Janet must observe, and certainly I will, if ever Janet has the child, that she never brings any other man, unless she's married to the bloke, home. As far as I'm concerned I want to be the father. If the baby's with me, and I was going out with some girl, I'm sorry, but Janet's her mother and that's the only girl she's going to see me with, unless I marry another woman.

'But, of course, if another man does come along and Janet does get married, what do I do? I don't know at the moment. I don't know what effect it's going to have if I continue to remain in the picture. I mean, he may not want me around. I see no reason why he should. O.K., he's got married to his wife and I'm just a stranger who keeps coming in and going out, looking after what is essentially his adopted child.

'Neither of us want to part with the kid, but then another thing is why should I just suddenly give her up like that? People are saying to me, *I* should have to give it up. Well, Christ, why shouldn't Janet give it up? You see? I mean, why should it be pointed at me, just because it's the way of our society?'

It is little understood that the distress experienced by men in this situation is by no means diminished because there are no real alternatives. Andrew has become deeply involved with his child and the threat of parting with her is, at present, unbearable. At the same time, he can clearly envisage the difficulties if Janet does marry, and probably knows that this will mean that he must remove himself from the situation. Therefore, he angrily criticizes society's assumption that he must be the one to give up the child. The simple answer to his rhetorical question is that since he has made no attempt to provide a home and security for his daughter, society must assume that she is better off with Janet. The confusion men experience at this stage in the situation, and the anger that confusion frequently arouses, stems from the fact that once a man rejects the normal alternatives to unmarried fatherhood, he does not have a leg to stand on.

His is a condition of impotence in the face of the inevitable, and the confused, often contradictory, nearly always vague alternatives put forward by the father should be seen as attempts to stave off an irrevocable and unpalatable decision.

Andrew's personal distress at the thought of parting from his child is perhaps aggravated by the fact that his lingering association with Janet, and the fact that his story is fairly widely known in the student community in which they both live, makes him virtually taboo to other girls. The moment a girl learns that he is, as he puts it, 'an unmarried daddy' she is unwilling to go out with him. 'They just don't want to know.' Andrew thinks this attitude arises from the fact that being known as an unmarried father lends a man a slightly dangerous, unreliable and disreputable reputation. It is also, I think, an example of female solidarity. A new girl friend is likely to have instinctive sympathy with Janet's situation and be unwilling to leave herself open to any criticism of having intervened in a relationship which might have a continuing future. Whatever the reason, Andrew is no longer regarded as a single man and is thus deprived of alternative female company which might give him a greater sense of perspective on his present situation. As it is, his emotions are entirely focussed on the child, for he freely admits that Janet no longer needs him.

Although he can envisage the possibility of Janet forming another relationship, he is loath to do so. Everything comes back, circular fashion, to the fact that he wants to be the child's father in more than the undisputed biological sense. Even his disagreements with Janet lead back to this point.

'When I come up and see them both, Janet says, "Give her toys to play with." You know, constant phrase ringing in my ears. "Give her toys to play with." Toys are only substitutes, as far as I can see, for me. Toys, fine, when she's by herself. When I'm there I don't want her to play with toys. I want her to take notice of me. I want her to look at my face, look at my hair, play with it. Fling her up and down in the air. She really enjoys that, you know? So it really is more normal if I am there.'

Like many other unmarried fathers, Andrew obviously derives a sense of importance and identity from being needed.

This is the key to his support of Janet and now that he recognizes that this no longer applies, he continually stresses the child's need of him.

This present state of irresolution is further complicated by the fact that Janet has considered emigrating. This Andrew sees as a more direct and immediate threat than the possibility of her marrying. Indeed, he takes the threat seriously enough to contemplate using unscrupulous methods to prevent any such move. Again we must recognize the admitted pattern of not wanting to let go.

'If she does emigrate, the baby's going to be two, maybe three. So I'll say, "Fair enough, Janet, off you go." I'll have to appeal to her guilty feelings. I mean, it's blackmail in a way. I don't want openly to have that kid used as blackmail between us. I mean, we could simply use that kid as a battle-ground and, God, that will destroy that kid quicker that anything else. But I'm going to say, "Look, the child's two or three. It knows me as its daddy. If you want to go off somewhere and destroy it, well, fine, off you go. You just stick the knife in." So at the moment I've got to play passive, regardless of whether I want to finish or not. Really it's like running an economy. A bit on this, a bit on that, and a bit on something else, to stretch the time at least until Janet has to realize that I have to be in the picture.

'Or I might say, "Look, Janet, I'll try and make the best of a bad job. Will you accept me marrying you?" Or I might say, yet again, "Look, Janet, I've tried my best and I don't think we'll get any further by continuing. And, you know, if you want to find someone else, I'll move out of the picture so you've got a completely free hand."

Although there is as yet no neat ending to Andrew's story, there is evidence, hopeful evidence, that he is beginning to assess the situation more objectively and to realize that the pattern of not wanting to let go must eventually be broken.

'She can't see life the way I see life, and I don't expect her to, but I'm trying to show her. And she says, "That doesn't exist. I can't see it." Because she hasn't experienced it. I've tried to give her my experience telescoped into a far shorter time. I think she's rather naïve, really. Far less so now than what she was when I met her. She's had a fair amount of experience, I think, the last twelve months or so. In a way, her own best friend is going to be her own mind, and I'm just going to leave it to think. I've been doing a lot of thinking for her in these last twelve months. She must think for herself in the next twelve months.'

Bill: A fortnightly father

'A bloke doesn't just think about beer, baccy and football. A bloke thinks just as much of his child as a woman does. I saw my daughter when she was forty-five seconds old and immediately fell in love with her.'

Carol-Anne sits on her father's knee throughout the interview. She is a pretty, lively baby, meticulously cared for. She is not at all overawed by strangers. My tape recorder attracts her gurgling attention intermittently, but there is no doubt that she prefers tugging at her father's hair and the beard he grew especially to amuse her. These games are punctuated by the little girl's laughter and entirely absorb the delighted man. After a time, she grows sleepy and snuggles down in her father's arms. She sleeps peacefully, her contented snuffling providing a ground bass to the conversation.

Unlike most mothers who spend all day and every day with their children, Bill has not developed the trick of ignoring his child while he talks. He is alert to her needs and doings, frequently interrupting himself to talk directly to her. At such times it is difficult not to feel like an intruder. The scene is one of such contentment, of security and affection that it is hard to believe that Carol-Anne's thirteen months of life have been so eventful. Yet, promptly at seven p.m., Bill will return his daughter to her foster parents, and will not see her again for a fortnight.

D

Bill and Carol-Anne's mother lived together for about a year. They were going to be married, but seven days before the wedding, the woman left him. Fifteen days after the birth of the baby, it was clear that the relationship was at an end. Bill immediately applied for custody of his daughter under the Guardianship of Minors Act, but the County Council took Carol-Anne into care. The mother's health at the time and the over-crowded conditions of the couple's home, with relatives, seem to have prompted this step. Bill's reaction was one of deep depression. In very quick succesion he had lost a woman he cared for and his daughter. His application to the Court met with a series of adjournments. Carol-Anne was moved straight from the maternity unit to a Children's Home. Bill continued to visit her there.

'I didn't feel easy there. I was made to feel as though I was a stranger. They just tolerated me. When she was still in hospital I got into the habit of ringing for information about her if I didn't go down to see her. Just to ask how she was. When she was in the Children's Home, I started to ring up and they complained because I was ringing them up every day. So I got restricted to two visits a week. I saw her for about an hour. At the beginning I wasn't allowed to hold her, but later on, yes.'

After nearly three months in the home, Carol-Anne was placed with foster parents.

'I was still trying to fight for custody of her before she went to the foster parents. As soon as she went to them and I met them I thought, Well, this seems the best solution at the moment to me. If I carried on with the summons, I wouldn't stand a chance anyway. The Court would automatically come down and say, Well, she's got a safe home, whereas I'm at work all day, no wife... Now she's with the foster parents she's being brought up in a very good home, with two other children, and I think she should stay there. If she went to her mother she would have no other children. Likewise, if she came to me she'd have no other children to play with. So I've rather got to thinking that she should stay with the foster parents. It's a question of what's best for the child. The Welfare always say they reckon that, but talking to them they always seem to say what's best for the mother. To me it's what's best for the child and, in my opinion, that is to be with the foster parents.'

Bill's experience of the Social Services department have been mixed and, to an observer, the root cause of the difficulty is a familiar one. Authoritative bodies which have to take steps to protect children in Carol-Anne's position are not prepared, mentally or administratively, for the presence of a concerned and responsible unmarried father. Bill 'rather hit 'em like a bombshell, actually. They weren't quite sure what to do.' In fact, this particular body seems to have coped better than most. Bill admits that 'they recognized my feelings towards my daughter and recognized the fact that I must have access to her.' As Bill appreciates, the fundamental problem is with the law.

'With illegitimate children, the mother's got all the rights and the father's got no rights. The only legal right I've got is that she's (Carol-Anne) got my name. In fact, when a child is taken into care, the law is that the mother should have an opportunity to object to that care order. The County Council gave written notification that a care order was there and asked for written objection from the mother. I was given no written notification and therefore couldn't object in writing.'

But if the law militates against the unmarried father, the people who are empowered by the law are also capable of acting in very devious ways.

'Before she was taken into care I said that I wanted her. They turned round and said, "Well, how can you look after her? You're not working." I was unemployed at the time. "You're not working. How can you support her? Get a job and you stand a much better chance." So I got a job and then they turned round and said to me, "You can't look after her. You're working all day." So I can't have her if I haven't got a job and I can't have her if I have got a job. So I can't win either way.'

By this time Bill was living with his parents who were considered too old to take on the responsibility of looking after a baby. Having got a job, however, he wanted to contribute to his child's maintenance. This involved him in a nine-month battle. 'It wasn't anything they said, it was just their attitude, you know? I found they were dragging their feet over it. All full of red tape and that.' Eventually, Bill threatened to come to a private financial arrangement with his daughter's foster parents and as a result, was allowed to pay a monthly sum to the County Council for her maintenance.

This account is, of course, one sided, but it is difficult to see why a man should not be encouraged to support his child when he is willing to do so, unless it is that by allowing him to pay it becomes more difficult to fob him off with *Catch-22* type arguments which in fact curtail his involvement. Since both Carol-Anne's parents refuse to entertain the idea of adoption, Bill's responsible insistence on giving financial help – quite apart from its importance to his pride – can scarcely complicate the situation. One is forced to conclude that the father is still regarded as an embarrassment, somebody who, because he has been traditionally excluded, represents a new and disturbing element in the smooth running of the department. Bill's active presence obviously makes the situation a triangular one, but feeling as he does about his daughter, there is no other possible way for him to behave. From the child's point of view the father's involvement simply swells the number of people concerned with its welfare. This may cause administrative problems, certainly requires that more arguments and considerations be carefully weighed, but the positive effect to the child must surely take precedence over such matters.

His lack of rights and the 'reluctance' of the Social Services to accommodate his involvement led Bill to start a press campaign designed to draw attention to the situation of unmarried fathers.

'I was getting absolutely frustrated not having any decision, not being allowed to take any decision about her whatsoever. So I wrote to the local paper about it and a chappy comes here and says it's too good for a letter, "Can we use it as a story?" I said, "Help yourself." They got it on the front page of the local paper. Well, the next thing I knew was a News Agency asked permission to put it in the national press.'

More newspaper stories followed as well as television appearances. At one stage, before the National Council for One Parent Families changed its scope and name, Bill advocated the need for an equivalent body, for fathers, to the National Council for the Unmarried Mother and Her Child. He thinks that the campaign has had a two-fold effect. Although the helping agencies would prefer him not to talk so freely to the press, the publicity has activated official sympathy for his case. He feels that social workers now have a greater understanding of his love and concern for Carol-Anne, and that they are trying to help him in many ways, such as obtaining more frequent access to his daughter. But easy as it is to heap blame on the Social Services, they too are affected by public opinion or, in this case, public ignorance. In this respect, the campaign has had a more general and perhaps a more important effect in so far as it reached ordinary, uninvolved people.

'People never seem to have thought of the problem. After reading about it and me telling them about it, they've all said I've made them stop and think. They've thought, Well, yes, a father should have the same rights as a mother. The law should be changed. It's a problem they never knew existed before. They've got so used to the idea that fathers of illegitimate children just run away and leave them that they've never come across it before. Strangely enough, I get the same attitude from women as I do from men – general support in the matter.

'Another reason why it's still not well known is, I think, because men are still basically a bit shy about coming forward and saying, "Yes, I'm the father of an illegitimate child and proud of it." I'm proud I'm her father. People seem surprised that I'm not ashamed in any way. But I can't see any reason to be ashamed. A lot of people have said to me, "We support you. We agree with everything you say, but we must admire your courage standing up in front of the whole country saying you're the father of an illegitimate child." Well, what's being brave about that? You know, I just can't understand their way of thinking. They think it takes bravery to do that. It's just natural. to stand up and say I want something to do with my daughter. A father like me is regarded a bit like an unmarried mother was about fifty years ago. My dad always says I shouldn't stand up and say I'm the father of an illegitimate child. He says there were no illegitimate children in his day. I tell him to pull the other one. There's been illegitimate children since the year dot, but nobody's stood up and talked about it before.'

Most heartening of all is the fact that thirty-six unmarried fathers wrote to Bill as a result of the publicity he received. They wrote to support him and to indicate that his experiences and his concern are not unprecedented.

Bill, however, is not sentimental about illegitimacy. Carol-

Anne carries his name and he does not anticipate that her status will create any major problems for her.

'Being illegitimate isn't anything special. There's nothing special about her. She's just like any other little kid. It's just that her Mum and Dad haven't got a wedding certificate.'

The specific message of Bill's campaign is to urge a simple change in the law.

'Broadly speaking, a law that gives a father of an illegitimate child the same rights as a normal married or divorced father. At the moment the law prevents a father like me having a say at all. The only law that goes half-way is the Guardianship of Minors Act, but there are some ifs, ands and buts in it.'

It is, as Bill's case demonstrates, often the interpretation of these 'ifs, ands and buts' which are most difficult to bear and which make a change in the law a matter of urgency and of commonsense.

Bill is very happy with the present fostering arrangements for Carol-Anne. The foster parents accept him and, perhaps because their knowledge of the case is personal and direct, they seem to understand his anxieties about his daughter and keep him reassured and informed. Ideally, Bill would like Carol-Anne to remain with her foster parents until she is grown up. He points out that theirs is the first home that she will remember. She has other children to play and grow up with. Equally important is the fact that he sees the foster home as neutral ground, an independent establishment where both he and the child's mother can have access to her without involving her in any wrangles or disagreements. Whether such a long-term fostering arrangement is possible it is difficult to say. Bill feels that the Social Services are rather against the idea and he contemplates coming to a private arrangement with the foster parents. This would depend, of course, on who eventually has custody of the child.

Both parents are agreed that adoption is not a possibility. Bill also recognizes that Carol-Anne's mother is concerned with her daughter and has to think about the possibility of her obtaining custody. This would depend on the Social Services satisfying themselves that she was well enough to cope and to provide a home. She has married since Carol-Anne's birth and

could, presumably, fill at least some of the requirements demanded by the authorities. Since Bill puts the mother's chances of
obtaining custody at fifty-fifty, what would his reaction be if
she succeeded?

'It's difficult to say, really. I suppose I would oppose it unless
I got guaranteed split custody, whereby I could have a say in
her future, regular contact with her and the right to information
about her. Basically, I want more than a divorced man, I think.
When you look at the bulk of divorce cases, the mother gets
custody of the children and what usually happens in practice is
that divorced men don't have a say in their child's welfare.
That's what I want, though. I want to be involved in her
welfare, informed when she's not well, consulted about her
education.'

Even if obtainable, a split custody order, giving dual responsibility to an estranged and unmarried couple, could lead to
difficulties. Bill thinks these are not insuperable and recognizes
the need for a family-type court.

'Again the law should enable parents who can't agree to
return to the law and say, "Well, what is the court's decision?
This or this?" But it would have to come to something really
major before that happened. I would think that if both parents
thought enough of the child, they would sit down and work out
something or other, some alternative compromise.'

Because of his anomalous legal and social position, the concerned unmarried father is invariably a prey to anxieties which,
objectively, one can see are likely to be a source of annoyance to
busy welfare agencies, but which are understandable when one
considers the impotence and frustration such men are bound to
feel. Nearly all the unmarried fathers who have contact with
their children whom I have met express an excessive concern
with the health of their children, for example. These are the
natural concerns of a father, exaggerated by limited contact and
the fear that they do not even have a right to know, to help.

In the light of this, it is easy to understand Bill's anxiety about
Carol-Anne's step-father. He points out that when fostering or
adoption are contemplated, a thorough investigation is made of
the 'parents' and their situation. No such investigation is
obligatory when a natural mother has married another man.
Bill wants reassurance that, in the event of Carol-Anne being

returned to her mother, the new husband will accept and love her. All sorts of possibilities go through his mind. Will she be resented? Will she always be regarded as another man's child? Such questions cannot easily be answered to the father's satisfaction. The newspaper spectre of Maria Caldwell haunts such people. Is the supervision of social care agencies adequate? How can one know with any certainty? Such anxieties are inevitably exaggerated by the tenuous recognition and limited rights of the unmarried father.

Bill rationally accepts that it is impossible for anyone to give him peace of mind on this point. The one thing that would reassure him is a meeting with the mother and her new husband to discuss the future and the way all three parties feel about it. At the time of our meeting, no such discussion had taken place, nor did one seem imminent. Even if it does occur it can never entirely remove the anxiety felt by men whose instinctive involvement with their children is constantly threatened by impersonal forces quite outside their control.

An attractive alternative would, of course, be for Bill to adopt his own daughter. Bill entertains no such hopes, and points to another legal anomaly.

'I would like to. The practicality there is the mother's objection. There again, if she objects, it stands in law. But if she wanted to adopt and I objected, that doesn't stand in law – which narks me. I'd like to see that changed.'

Bill, however, does not see himself as a life-long bachelor. At twenty-eight, the chances of him marrying are strong. Would he not then want to have Carol-Anne to live with him?

'Well, I've thought about this. I've thought about this a tremendous lot. To me, she would still be better off with her foster parents. She's known them ever since she can remember. She's been brought up with two kids there. They can guarantee her a stable home, somewhere independent where both I and her mother can have access to her, where both of us know that she is being very well looked after.'

To an extent, Bill is still emotionally involved with Carol-Anne's mother. Losing her on the eve of marriage was a shock. He still 'thinks a lot of her' but accepts that there is no future in that relationship. He would welcome the chance to form another but there are unexpected difficulties.

'The greatest problem is that I accept Carol-Anne and I want to accept her. I knock about with a few girls but they can't accept that I've got a daughter. Now some have made me choose between my daughter and them. I found no difficulty in choosing. I'll choose my daughter every time. I find that they don't want to know somebody else's child, and for me that's not a very good situation. In other words, if a girl accepts me, she's got to accept my daughter as well. She must accept that my love will be shared between her and my daughter.'

Perhaps this feminine attitude, which he thinks is partly explained by fear of his carrying a continuing torch for the mother of his child, has influenced his feeling that Carol-Anne, no matter what happens, will be better off with her foster parents, supplemented by regular contact with both her natural parents.

Bill is an attentive and capable parent, announcing as his daughter stirs awake that her nappy needs changing.

'The Welfare seemed surprised and rather disbelieving when I told them anything a woman can do for a baby I can do. I change her, feed her, bath her, give her love, play with her. When she's not feeling well, I know what to do with her. I I enjoy all that tremendously. Like when I changed her earlier. She had an absolutely filthy nappy, smelling to high heaven. To me, that was something that had to be done, so I didn't mind doing it.'

His fingers are stained with nicotine yet we have spent a cigarette-less afternoon in his parents' front room, where sweet-smelling apples are laid out on sheets of newspaper for winter storage. Bill has taken recent medical reports on the hazard to children of breathing in a smoke-laden atmosphere to heart. He never smokes in front of the baby and nags his social worker to prevent Carol-Anne's mother from doing so. Such caring responsibility is rare in parents at the best of times. With Bill it appears to be instinctive and is certainly genuine.

As I prepare to leave, Carol-Anne becomes absorbed in her own reflection in the mirror, prodding the image with tiny, exploring fingers. Wistfully, perhaps because his once-a-fortnight day of fatherhood is drawing to a close, Bill confides:

'The greatest thing I shall miss with her is one thing I looked forward to even before she was on the way. That is, sitting down and teaching her to read. I shall miss that because I should have enjoyed doing that. Even one day a week isn't enough. I'd like to sit down every day and try to teach her to read.'

Peter: Future ways

For an increasing number of men, unmarried fatherhood is a natural result of their rational rejection of marriage. Although, of course, unplanned pregnancies still occur in, for example, long-lasting affairs, such men are not faced with the same problems as the 'classic' unmarried father. Fatherhood is a contingency they have considered and is very often an important element in the relationships they have. They are, in one sense, unmarried fathers only in the technical meaning of the phrase, and that more or less by choice. Theirs is an alternative lifestyle. They do not believe in marriage and are more realistic – or pessimistic, depending on one's point of view – about the feasibility of one man being faithful to and content with one woman for a virtual lifetime. They certainly reject the idea that a marriage license has any power to influence their willingness to accept responsibility for their children, while the stigma of illegitimacy is something that exists only in the eyes of a conformist society.

Peter may be regarded as a case in point. His situation is, of course, quite individual, but some of his views are widely held. He lived with Sally for nearly six years. She was pregnant by another man when they met and Peter regards her son as his own child. Subsequently, she bore Peter a daughter and, although he is no longer living with them, he visits regularly and supports the children on a voluntary basis. Peter is living with another woman who is expecting his baby. She was married and has a child of her own. All the children know about and are involved in this pregnancy and are very excited that the new baby will relate them all.

Peter is in his early thirties, handsome, self-confident and well-dressed. In keeping with his situation he, unlike many other unmarried fathers to whom I have talked, had no need to unburden himself. He simply gave information and was willing to discuss his point of view.

BARBER: Sally was pregnant when you began living with her. How did you feel about this, and the second pregnancy?

PETER: My attitude to the first was. . . I quite accepted it. I mean it didn't aggravate me in any way. My attitude to the second was more extreme because I felt I'd really got a little bit trapped by that. Trapped in a relationship which I didn't want, necessarily, to be. Trapped, also, because of the first as well, because I accepted that as my own. The second seemed to confirm it. I'd got one child born biologically, and yet I'd got two. Though it didn't diminish my liking for the child.

B: You're no longer living here yet you voluntarily support these children. Do you resent that?

P: No, not at all, because, you know, to support them is to keep in touch, ties them to me. And I want to, anyway. it seems natural as long as I can afford to do it.

B: And how do you envisage this situation developing?

P: Over a period of years? Well, at the moment I see the kids for about half an hour three evenings a week, baby-sit one night a week and usually see them more or less the whole day Sunday. That pattern, I imagine, will be fairly constant until Sally lives with someone else.

B: Do you feel at risk because if Sally forms another relationship the man might take on the kids much as you took on Sally's son?

P: No. The kids are tied to me by knowing me and me being around. I'm not going to be alienated in their affections. The only problem will be if the man resents me coming round or whatever. We'll have to work this out between us. It becomes a question well, not of force, but of will.

B: In fact you're optimistic about this possibility?

P: I see no reason why I shouldn't be because I think whoever Sally is likely to live with should conceivably be considerate towards the children, enough to let me see them. And if he's not then it's up to me to do something about that. He may well think that I'm here too much, seeing the children too often. He may think it's best for the children not to see me, which I won't accept and will have to sort out.

B: Do you worry about the fact that your children are illegitimate?

P: I think it's great. That's putting it very badly and stupidly but. . . I totally disagree with Christian ethics and so therefore I consider illegitimacy to be a manufactured piece of propagandist nonsense. I think the only people who are likely to cause a problem in that respect are people who aren't worth worrying about at all. The children must learn to live with that. I mean I had to learn to live with certain things. You find out later that the things these people put in your path aren't really important. I have been taxed with that before. 'What about when they call them bastards?' Well, you get called a lot of things. You get called a lot of things if you're black. You've got to alter the attitudes of people who are saying that sort of thing. It's not going to be done by everybody paying lip-service to it all the time. And I think it's up to me to tell the kids that.

B: So you will explain their situation to them in those terms?

P: No. Things come up from day to day. I don't think you have to make a big issue of it. They'll say, 'When did you get married?' or something. You say, 'We're not. Some people do and some people don't.' You treat it as a matter of fact which, to me, it is. You just say, 'We chose to live together and that's the way it is.'

B: But isn't it complicated by the fact that you're no longer living with their mother?

P: It's complicated a little. Maybe. That's all I can say. You just fight things as you find them. I consider myself articulate enough to explain to them how I feel about things. It's up to them, then, whose moral judgement they take.

B: The important thing is that they shouldn't be told a lot of fairy stories?

P: Precisely. I don't know what fairy stories I'd tell them anyway. I don't think about it in those terms. I never think about explaining it to them because that'd make it seem as though I thought there was something bad about it. I don't believe and I don't subscribe to the Christian view of marriage. I've always lived among people who are either living together, or don't care, or got married and wished they hadn't, or got married because their parents wanted them to. In London you haven't got a family situation. Not many people I know live in close proximity to their families. So you've destroyed that. You've destroyed all the moral pressure there. You live in a society where people have done different things, and it's not a society with many virgins. You know, basically that's where it's at. Once you've destroyed the myth, that reality of the virgin bride and the clean-living boy who's had a few sexual encounters but is still basically very nice. . . Once you've destroyed that, there's absolutely no reason why you should take up the stupidity of the Christian marriage. Then a lot of people still have this attitude that you live together until you have a child and then you get married *for* the child. I can understand that, but I think it's silly because the thing is just going to be perpetuated by that attitude. I've got great respect for people who manage to keep a marriage going. That's one way of living. I don't think it's the only way to live.

B: What sort of background do you come from?

P: Socially? Working-class I suppose you'd say. I've got two brothers and one sort of half-brother – all younger. My mother was divorced when I was very young and then married again later on. Now she's divorced him as well. I despised him. He was a peasant. We used to go and see my father for a while. It didn't last very long. I can just vaguely remember my father in those days and then I can remember just being bored out of my mind just being with him. I just don't remember doing anything. My relationship with my mother is reasonable. Reasonable. I can't communicate with her very well, but she's all right. I left home just before I was sixteen.

B: Did you receive any sex education at home or at school?

P: No.

B: Would you educate your own children sexually?

P: Oh yes. It doesn't worry me, but you can see so many problems. I know we all went through problems. . . I don't know what's best. Whether you keep problems and enjoy them. . . It was very nice experimenting, I must say. Very nice finding out. On the other hand I'll let the kids know what happens. Both of them know precisely how a child is conceived and born. And that's the only way it's got to be. It's got to be a natural thing. If they want to know something else, they can be told. There's nothing they can't be told.

B: But would you agree that not having any sex education was a hang-up?

P: First of all it was. You see, when I was ten I went away to a public school, so I was then segregated from women until I was fourteen. It was a problem, yes. I've got problems with relationships really. I still feel this. I'm much harder than most men. That may just be a personality thing. It doesn't worry me. When I was about fifteen, you see, I made a girl pregnant because I didn't know what the hell was going on. It was ridiculous. She had a miscarriage very early on. I was just worried. But it was ridiculous. Ludicrous. It could have ruined my life and it could have ruined hers, which is very silly at that stage. It ties in with sex education because of birth control.

B: Would you have welcomed information about birth control at fifteen?

P: Not when I was fifteen. I think it would have made things worse. I just think I'd have been embarrassed about the whole thing. It should be part of your equipment. It should be an automatic thing. I'm sure it's going to be automatic with these kids. They're never going to question it.

B: Is there a connection, do you think, between your being shut up at boarding school for four years and the difficulty you say you have with relationships now?

P: I don't mean now, I mean all the way through. I don't know. I'm very detached in general and in relationships in particular. I always consider that I'm outside all the time. I'm not very warm, which I think may be partly to do with that.

B: Did you have a sense of women as totally alien creatures about whom you knew nothing?

P: I think so, yes. That's probably overdoing it, but yes, I'm not sure that it isn't true now.

B: Well, did they scare you or did you want to find out as much as possible as quickly as possible?

P: Probably a bit of both. I think they were certainly held in awe, or discussed in wonder.

B: And how do you see women now?

P: Now? Foe. I regard the vast majority of them as a waste because really, you know, they're pretty thick. The vast, vast majority. I think they're even thicker than men, which is saying something. It may be for sociological reasons because they have been told all their lives that they're going to make some man happy, but I find them crushingly boring. I mean, you do find exceptions, obviously, but they are pretty rare. I think that's one of the problems we have today. You know, men would rather be with men and so would women. But it may be just biological. I enjoy their company to a certain extent, but if I'm feeling serious or humorous I generally prefer the company of men.

B: Earlier you spoke of being trapped when the second baby was coming. What do you mean by that exactly?

P: Trapped in some social prison that you don't really want to be in. A sort of programming. As though you've been plugged in. But, on the other hand, there's a deeper kind of prison, which is some sort of arriving at something you didn't want to arrive at. Actually being too involved. You're very conscious, if you like, of your responsibilities. I don't necessarily call them responsibilities. Your horizons seem just to disappear. There is also the situation of being tied to a child, emotionally. This doesn't really strike you when the child's conceived but suddenly, after it's born, you're emotionally tied. You want what is best for it and that may conflict with what is best for you. The two aren't easily reconciled sometimes. I'm very involved with the kids. I know I'm much less rigid with them than I am with somebody else – which is a kind of trap. I accept it now. I like it. But when Sally was first pregnant it was a kind of panic. Not because of any irresponsibility, but just because it was some social situation one didn't necessarily want to be in at that particular time.

B: So would you say that your emotional attachment to the children is stronger than to any woman?

P: If I said 'yes' then your question to me afterwards would be, Why aren't I with the children rather than with a woman?

B: No. I was referring to this idea that men aren't supposed to be very emotionally committed to their children and wondering, since you are very fond of yours, if you could differentiate between that and your emotional attachment to women.

P: Well, with the kids there's no competition, if you like. They're totally demanding but totally loyal in their own way. They're totally attached to you. There's no question. Well, they're critical in some ways, but they're non-discriminatory. I suppose my emotional attachment to the children is much greater than the emotional attachment I give to any woman. Obviously because they need it, I give the kids a much sounder emotional basis for their relationship with me than I do to a woman.

B: Because they need it, not you?

P: I think I probably do as well. Because they're part of me. They're a reassurance, if you like.

B: Of what? Your existence?

P: Maybe. I don't know. They're just there. It's nice that they are there. I've always found that men like children much more than women do. Women see children as a triumph. It's something to do with *them* – do you know what I mean?

B: Women try to make children an extension of their own personalities?

P: I was accused of doing that. Trying to make the children an extension af myself. I think I do, to a certain extent. But it's a question of you having to look around and decide who the kids are to be like, and you want them to be like you. I'm accused of sort of trying to make their minds up for them. I consider there's a lot of pressures from outside on different things, so I exert a little pressure from the other side. Like this Jesus thing. They get so much crap shoved down their throats about Jesus at school – in a nice way – so I see no reason why I shouldn't give them a little bit of pushing from the other side. Not making them a battleground, but they've got to know that there are people who think differently.

B: Another big difference between a man's and a woman's attitude to children, I think, is that men really can survive without their children.

P: Yes. Women say they can't but if they've got to, they will. You see, in all relations of this kind, and in married relations as well, the man is in a very inferior position because he can't say, 'O.k. I'll have the kids and go and live on supplementary benefit' – which maybe one would like to do. But the woman can always say, 'O.K. I'm off. I'll take the kids' and there's very little you can do about it. I suppose that's reasonable in this society because women do spend most time with them. But if they're saying they can't live without them, that's rubbish, because men have to and I'm sure men's feelings towards their children are just as strong. It's just the social situation that men work and women have childen. That's the only reason that it's got currency. People think – I have come across this – that because you're not married and don't live with the kids, that you're letting them down. Or that you're very clever. Men think you're very clever. 'Oh yes, that's great. Brilliant. If only I could do that.' But in fact you're in quite a bad position with the kids really. Because – and I have thought about this – if Sally forms another relationship, she could very easily get a court order to say I shouldn't see them. Now that's perfectly within a judge's scope, if he considers it to be bad for the children. I don't think it'll happen in this case, but I do think it's something that ought to be changed.

B: You'd welcome some sort of automatic right of access for unmarried fathers, then?

B: Definitely.

B: As far as your child was concerned, did you ever contemplate abortion or adoption?

P: Both. Because basically being not an unwanted child but an unwanted foetus – draw that distinction – it was contemplated by both of us because we weren't having a very good time and we thought it would be the best thing. Then, just when the baby was born Sally decided she was going to keep her. Then, well, we went back together again because it just seemed the most sensible thing to do. I must say I've never regretted that. Once you see the child – I saw the child in the hospital and I didn't see it. You know what I mean? I deliberately put the shutters down. But as soon as I actually saw it, I never regretted a minute of it.

B: So how would you define your particular situation with the kids?

P: I don't know. It's **very** difficult to define, but I know when they're away they want to come back and see me. That's all. I want to see them. That's really the relationship we have. They rely on me for certain things – like money. I think I'm probably

special to them and they're special to me. I have a bit to say with
what they do, but it's nothing heavy.

B: Doesn't that sort of relationship depend on one's instinctive
ability to think of children as people?

P: Maybe, Yes. I was asked the other day why I don't speak to
people like I do to the kids. 'You change when you speak to the
kids. Why don't you speak to women like that?' The only thing
I could say was that they were the only people who deserve it.
They're unmoulded clay. Everyone else has gone too far. I don't
know, perhaps it's just that I'm too competitive. I feel I can be
gentle with them. It's gentleness with them whereas it would be
weakness if I did it to other people. It gives me the opportunity
to be gentle to someone, I suppose. I think maybe I don't see
them as people.

B: You obviously mistrust people.

P: Oh I'm very wary.

B: Why?

P: Because they're not worthy of trust, basically.

B: Is that view based on actual experience?

P: No, I don't think so. It's just instinctive. I don't really trust
people too far. Women less than men. I don't trust them to be
straight with me. I just have an instinctive separation. I always
like to be in the driver's seat. I always like to know where I'm
going and that I'm in control of the car, so that at any given
moment I can turn off. It's a question of being threatened. I
don't want anyone to feel that they are getting one up on me.
With the children you know that they are no threat in that
respect.

B: Do you think that this sense of mistrust and detachment
stems from your background as the eldest son, and being sent
away to school?

P: It may have been. My mother was living in one room in the
same place as my father, but on her own, and I found I was in
some sort of role of helping to look after the kids, avoiding the
tallymen. I suppose it all helps. But you survive. Other people
go down. She only sent me to boarding school because I was the
most intelligent and passed the exam. I can understand what
they thought. The English Public School has always appeared
to be a great place to send your child if you could, so I think
they thought they were doing me a favour. I was one of the only

two non-fee-paying boys there, so that gave me a sense of my own superiority.

B: Do you think a man in your position, someone who has rejected traditional marriage has to be more aware of the problems of having children than a man who conforms to the usual pattern?

P: Yes, I think so. I think you *are* more aware anyway because you've thought about doing the thing in the first place. Once you've accepted the child you've thought about it a certain amount. More than the father does when he's married. It's just an automatic thing, then. But I think you've got to be very aware of the child. You've got to really make sure it knows it's wanted, because otherwise the presumption is around that it's not wanted. Which is a lie. No, I really love them. I certainly don't regret having them.

B: Would you say, then, that there is such a thing as a paternal impulse?

P: You mean a Lawrentian movement towards your children? A seeking to have children? Yes. I think there is. I'd certainly say I've got it. It's not as obsessive as a woman's theoretical urge. I always thought it would be nice to have children. I thought that when I saw men out with children in the park. But you go through all these different stages. After the child's born – it's this horrid little bundle. Revolting little thing. So then it's just there and you like it. But then, when they're a year, they're incredible. I don't think the paternal instinct is as strong as the maternal instinct, but there is a certain going towards it. It's not mystic. There's no denying that the woman's had the child. There's a physical feeling of it. I could have had my daughter adopted before she was my daughter. I would have felt bad about it, but I certainly could have. She wouldn't really have existed for me. But once having had her for two or three months, I would never have considered it. With a man it grows afterwards. A woman's more physically involved the whole time. It's perfectly possible to father a child and not know, or decide not to be involved. But I'm sure you have a thought about it years later. 'I wonder what's happened to that child?' I know the father of Sally's son and he's never mentioned it. He's not interested at all. I don't think he's that way inclined, which is just as well in this particular case. He's never seen him. He doesn't seem to want to. I presume. But as I say, he will, probably in twenty or thirty years' time. Just imagine, to have something of you walking around and not to want to see what they look like. How they turned out. Extraordinary!

Part two

'The very obvious fact that for every unwed mother there is an unwed father has been virtually ignored by social agencies and the helping professions. We have failed to see him as a person with feelings, sensitivities, in need of help. We have wrongly assumed that he is not concerned with the woman he impregnates or her offspring.'

Reuben Pannor, *The Unmarried Father - The Forgotten Man*

Lecture delivered to the National Coucil for the Unmarried Mother and Her Child (now One Parent Families) 1971

Introduction

It will already be apparent that the stereotype is too general, too simple to have any practical usefulness in understanding the unmarried father. Even those interviewees who might conceivably approximate to the model do so only in the most general terms and then at the expense of individual factors which contributed to their situation and influenced their response to it. The bulk of these men, however, represent the committed, concerned fathers, those for whom responsibility is a very real and lively matter. After their individual problems, their most pressing concern is with the law, how it affects them and how it might be improved to their advantage. In the interviews themselves, some of the inadequacies have been glimpsed in action. However, a proper examination of the law and the possibility of improving it is essential.

As we shall see, the law only represents existing social attitudes. It seems to me therefore obvious that the lot of the committed unmarried father will be proportionately improved if society at large takes a more concerned and helpful attitude towards unmarried fathers in general. Relying very heavily on the work done in California at the *Vista Del Mar* Child-Care Service, I have tried to describe how such helping approaches may be made and what we and, more importantly, the fathers may be expected to gain therefrom.

The *Vista Del Mar* work focuses our attention on another group of fathers – young representatives of the 'red-blooded youth' syndrome. They are, in many ways, very different from the interviewees, but what is interesting is the way in which many of them came to play a caring, responsible role towards the mother and child after being recipients of the new approaches.

Underlying the whole problem of illegitimacy is the failure of unwed potential parents to practise contraception. I believe this is a particularly distressing failure when the unmarried parents are very young. From their attitudes and difficulties, however, we can perhaps discover something about the general reluctance to practise contraception in situations which are likely to cause an illegitimate birth.

Finally, I think it is important to say something about the great majority of men, the silent stereotype of an unmarried father who is conspicuous by his absence. One can, in fact, say very little about him with any authority, but I believe there is a responsibility to consider his apparent point of view and to question whether helping agencies and society as a whole have any right to seek to alter his behaviour.

The Unmarried Father and the Law

The law does not discriminate against unmarried fathers as such. It simply experiences great difficulty in seeing them as anything other than the reluctant recipients of Affiliation Orders.

It is a truism worth repeating, that the law follows in the wake of public opinion – and not merely out of laggard perversity, either. The ideal of the law is that any citizen should, at any time, be able to understand the laws to which he or she is subject. Pipe dream that this is, it must mean that changes in social attitudes lead the way. That these occur slowly is obvious to everyone. The law is even slower to reflect them because of its necessary idealism. Pettifogging as the principle may appear to those who suffer from the law's slow rate of change, it is a principle few people would care to see discarded.

It is important to establish that the manifold inadequacies in the law as it concerns putative fathers today, were not deliberately designed, nor, indeed, are the courts to blame for them. Courts are only concerned to enforce existing laws, and the relevant ones are adequate to the traditional needs and views of the unmarried father. Society's opinion was that by refusing to marry the mother of his natural child, the father was declaring his intention to disassociate himself as completely as possible from the situation. Few people, I think, would argue that the law should not then do what little it can to provide for the maintenance of the child. These laws were formed at a time when the idea of any father, let alone an unmarried one, being anything more than a provider and a disciplinarian was unthinkable, and when men as a sex had virtually no opportunity to assume any sort of day-to-day responsibility for their children. Although the provision of state payments and day care centres is inadequate, their existence does provide men with the possibility of assuming daily responsibility for their children. Even today, however, the portion of society which sees a need for revision or amendment, which accepts that fathers should have the right to choose full responsibility for their natural children, is a minority.

The present state of affairs is, in fact, an excellent illustration of the law lagging behind public opinion, but it would be unrealistic to pretend that public opinion, or indeed the vast majority of fathers themselves, are urging a change in the law. Although the precedent of putative father's rights has been clearly established at law, the demand for them is by no means so great that the courts or legislators can be accused of resistance.

This apparent satisfaction with the *status quo* is not, of course, an argument against reform and revision. There is already a minority of men who do desire such changes, but more importantly they can be urged in the name of the child, for whose protection they are designed.

An anomaly in the law, even if it only affects one person, is cause for concern, and in a period of slow revision of attitudes to unmarried fathers it becomes a matter of considerable importance. These anomalies are, however, frequently compounded by assumptions, legal and human, which greatly influence the attitude and deliberations of a court of law. Therefore, it would be true to say that although the putative father has certain rights under existing law, neither professional nor lay opinion is used to his exercising these rights. The quality of surprise experienced by a court faced with a father seeking to establish his rights to have care and control of his child will be aggravated by traditional attitudes. Why does this man, having made his position quite clear by refusing to marry the mother, want to swim against the tide of traditional masculine behaviour? Does not his sex and the demands of society upon his sex make him ill-equipped to care for a child? Has his behaviour not already indicated his unreliability, his non-conformity? Is such a person fit to care for a child, even if he can do so? Is there not perhaps some ulterior motive lurking behind his application to the court?

The very fact that a significant number of men have exercised their just rights over their natural children is proof in itself that these assumptions do not influence every court. Hurtful and demeaning as they are to the distressed father who is trying to balance his feeling of love and responsibility towards his child with his own needs as a man, few people, I think, would attack a court for taking some of these questions into consideration when the future well-being of a vulnerable child is at stake. A man who is sufficiently determined to go through the compara- tively unknown and therefore risky processes of law necessary to obtain any realistic form of influence over his natural child may be expected to weather these assumptions. What are more alarming are the legal assumptions about the putative father, and their considerable power to discourage men who feel a genuine and constructive involvement with their children.

A married male parent, seeking divorce or separation, is automatically regarded as joint guardian and custodian of the child. Until the court decides otherwise. No Decree Nisi can be declared absolute until the court is satisfied that arrangements for the child are at least adequate and preferably suitable. The Judge has a duty, no matter how amicably uncontested the divorce, to satisfy himself that the best conditions possible have been secured for the child and a set document concerning this aspect of the case has to be submitted. If the child is to reside with the mother, it is naturally assumed that the father has right of access, unless there is some powerful reason for the court to decide other- wise. Similarly, a divorced woman has an established right to maintenance for her child and would usually have a right to personal maintenance. These rights, affecting both parties and centrally concerned with the child's well-being, are an accepted part of divorce proceedings and are dealt with by one court and at one time.

Where unmarried parents are concerned – and the law here makes no distinction between the couple who have cohabited for a period of years, bringing up their children in a family situation, and the abandoned mother who has never had an ongoing, stable relationship with the man – the law assumes that the mother is the legal guardian, parent and custodian of the natural child. Since she faces the identical responsibilities at law towards her child as any married parent, it may be argued that this assumption contains a certain rough justice. On the other hand she has no rights to maintenance for herself. She can apply for maintenance of her child only, and the operative word here is 'apply'. The father is assumed to have no rights, only a responsibility to contribute towards his child's maintenance, once paternity has been established.

These matters are decided under Affiliation Proceedings which are cruelly simple. The function of the court is to establish paternity and to obtain maintenance for the child. Affiliation Proceedings are in no way concerned with the rights of the putative father. Even more alarming is the fact that the court granting an Affiliation Order is not concerned as to whether the arrangements provided for the child are satisfactory. A father who wants to exercise normal rights over his child, who may feel that the mother is an unfit person to have custodianship of the child can do nothing about it under Affiliation Proceedings. In such cases, however, the majority of courts would inform and concern themselves with the child's circumstances which might, in time, lead to the father's greater involvement. Certainly it would afford protection to the child.

Paternity is considered to be established on the evidence of the mother, provided that evidence is corroborated either by written or by verbal testimony. The supposed father can insist upon blood tests being taken and the mother has a right to refuse. If she does so on any grounds other than religious ones, the court may well infer from this that she is making a false accusation. The blood test, however, is a negative proof. It can establish only that a given man cannot be the father of a given child. It cannot establish positive paternity.

Once paternity is decided, to the satisfaction of the court, an Affiliation Order is made which requires the man to pay a certain sum to the mother for the upkeep of his child. It is at this point that we encounter one of those circular inanities which seem to bedevil certain areas of the law to the detriment of those it is designed to help. The accent is placed, in effect, on payment of money rather than on the future importance of paternity to the child. Many far-sighted women would like to establish paternity for the sake of their children. One would think that Affiliation Proceedings could establish this and enable the woman to waive maintenance. This is not so. A court will not grant an Affiliation Order unless it entails the payment of an agreed sum. The woman can, of course, ask for a purely nominal sum, but she automatically has the right to apply at any time to the court to reassess this amount and have it scaled up to a realistic figure. Consequently, many putative fathers are encouraged to deny paternity because they place themselves at possible future financial risk. An atmosphere of mutual mistrust is fostered between the parents, and the child may never be able to legally establish the facts of his paternity.

Affiliation Proceedings were established to help the mother and child financially, but they also embody the punitive idea that the man must pay for his pleasure. They grant the father no rights. He has merely the protection of having to have his paternity proven. Once that is achieved, he has to pay up. It cannot, therefore, be a matter of great surprise that men are reluctant to admit paternity, that they regard the whole proceedings as being favourable to greedy women. The very process of law encourages the separation of mother, father and child and it does so by requiring a woman to enter a criminal court and 'prove' that she has had sexual intercourse with a certain man on certain dates. Is it any wonder that so many women would rather put up with hardship than undergo such a trial, even though this means that her child may never be able legally to recognize his father? And who can argue with the putative father who said, when his paternity was not proven, 'They didn't find me guilty, then'?

Clearly there is one law for the married man and woman and one for the unmarried, when they are parents. Those who make a responsible, conscious choice not to marry, or who cannot marry, are subject to the same process of law as those who fulfil the more popular idea of unmarried parents. Obviously it is unrealistic to expect courts to make fine distinctions between those who have cohabited over a long period and the casual, isolated sexual act which results in a baby being born out of wedlock, but it is difficult to see why the unmarried parent should be treated so very differently.

While we have no choice but to accept that the majority of

unmarried fathers are quite content with the law, providing they can evade Affiliation Proceedings, there remains the increasing number of men who want to exercise some degree of control over their children and to establish a relationship with them. What can a man who feels this way do? Certainly Affiliation Proceedings cannot help him and must, in any case, be brought by the mother.

The best way a putative father can seek to establish his right is to apply to the court on summons under the Guardianship of Minors Act for access, custody or care and control. Obviously, he will have to establish paternity in the first place, and this can be done by a simple admission of the fact. Access is simply the right, granted automatically to divorced or separated fathers, to see the child. A court will normally make an order for reasonable access which leaves the parents free to make detailed arrangements. If this breaks down the court will, reluctantly, specify times and frequency.

Custody is the right to influence and play a part in the arrangements for and future of the child. Normally, custody is granted with the more far-reaching care and control, but in the case of an unmarried father, custody alone might take on a more important role. It is possible, for example, for a man to wish to be consulted about the child's education or living arrangements even though he could not provide a home himself for the child. Therefore custody, without care and control, would be a valuable gain.

Care and control on the other hand places the child in that parent's control. He or she becomes the parent with whom the child normally resides, and who is entirely responsible for the child on all counts.

A summons taken out under the Guardianship of Minors Act can theoretically establish the putative father's right of access, to custody and care and control. Theoretically because there is nothing in the letter of the law that denies him these rights. He, however, has to take the initiative and the burden is squarely placed on his shoulders to show that the child needs or should see him, or requires to be placed in his care.

Mr Stephen Lloyd, a lawyer and a member of the National Council for One Parent Families (formerly NCUMC), points to the existence of a gap between this theory and the practise.

It can be definitely stated that because there is not a habit in our society of the man taking an interest, it is a very uphill task for him to get even an access order, let alone a custody or care and control order. There is still a tremendous feeling in our society – very wrongly in my view – of an almost proprietary right on the part of the unmarried mother to have charge and control of her child. It's *her* child. *He* landed her with the problem. The man really has got to convince the court that he should be allowed to see the child. In some courts, I suspect, there is almost a feeling that he is an undesirable person *per se* and would be a bad influence on the child anyway. On the other hand, I think nearly all matrimonial courts would assume that the father had a right to access unless the mother could show that he was an undesirable person. If a man is applying for access to a child of whom he is the putative father, the burden is on him to show that the child should see him. That is not the rule in law at all. In law his rights to access are the same as a married father's but I am certain that in practise they are very hard to obtain.

In fact the most persuasive grounds for making such an application are that the mother is in some way an unfit person to have care and control of the child. This, of course, completely rules out any chance of obtaining custody alone since no court is going to accept the influence of an unmarried father who maintains that the child is living with an unfit person. Application would therefore be made for custody and care and control. It is enormously difficult for the father who (a) has no criticism of the child's home circumstances and mother but (b) would like to be consulted about major decisions affecting the child's future and well-being to obtain custody alone.

Again the law, without malice, is effectively driving a wedge between putative father and offspring. The assumption that by refusing to marry the mother the man has abrogated all the usual rights of a parent is unavoidable. However, putative fathers have been successful under the Guardianship of Minors Act and it remains the most hopeful form of redress open to men who do not accept that the absence of marriage automatically entails total disassociation from their children.

There are two other ways in which the unmarried father can seek to establish his right to be involved with his child. They

E

involve many more risks of failure and are much more expensive than proceedings under the Guardianship of Minors Act. Perhaps more importantly, they seem to have, if successful, only a limited efficacy from the father's point of view and would seem to be applicable only in very exceptional circumstances. Given the attitude of the courts, it is unlikely that they will provide a father with real involvement with his child.

Although the procedure was never intended for this purpose it is possible to have the natural child made a Ward of Court. In that case the court will assume custody of the child and, since it obviously has no facilities for the care of children, will make a care and control order in favour of whoever the court decides is a fit person. This could be mother or father, or some other relative such as a grandparent. The court may, however, decide to place the child in the care of the local authority. Ward of Court proceedings are obviously a roundabout route for the father who wishes to exercise control over his child. The effective decision-making process remains in the hands of the court and the father would, in the face of the sort of opposition already discussed, have to persuade the court that he was the right person to have care and control.

If, however, the father did not wish or was unable to assume full guardianship of the child, but wanted to ensure that the child remained within the jurisdiction of the court, then these proceedings could be effective. The aim of Ward of Court proceedings is essentially to prevent British minors, irrespective of age, being taken out of the country. Wardship might also be obtained if the father could show that the child was in some imminent and real danger. Thus if the mother were a foreign national, or planning to emigrate, then such proceedings might prove very effective indeed. It is, however, extremely unlikely that a father would obtain care and control by this process, and certainly if that is his prime aim, application under the Guardianship of Minors Act would be much more sensible.

There is a third method of approach. Superficially, it is very attractive and can solve the problem of a father who wishes to protect rather than obtain legal guardianship of his child. Obviously, there are situations when the latter goal is quite unrealistic but when the child's circumstances are such as to excite the father's concern. If the child is in danger, either physical or moral danger, he can approach the local Social Services Department or the Children's Department of his local authority and ask them to apply for a Fit Person's Order, by which process the child will be taken into care. Care and control is then, as it were, in the gift of the relevant department. In law there is nothing to prevent care and control being given to the father but in practise it is unlikely. Once involved, the Social Services Departments invariably feel that they have a responsibility to care for the child. The same prejudices and assumptions about the single father will apply perhaps even more strongly. Therefore paternal guardianship is a possibility but far from being a certainty. This procedure obviously has distinct advantages for the endangered child whose father either does not wish or is unable to provide a home and daily care for the child.

Ward of Court and Fit Persons Proceedings have very limited efficacy as far as the committed father is concerned, although they may fit a different bill quite admirably. The father who wishes access, or custody and care and control, would be well advised to invoke the Guardianship of Minors Act. It is a quick and efficient method of procedure. It is heard in a local Magistrate's Court – Ward of Court cases are heard in the High Court, which can create problems of travelling, time etc. – and legal aid can be applied for. Above all a summons issued under the Guardianship of Minors Act has the crucial advantage of defining exactly what the father wants to achieve. In either of the other procedures the father is placing himself entirely in the hands of the court or the local authority. They make decisions about care and control, whereas by the former procedure the court is bound to award custody to one or other of the parties in contention.

It must be stressed that a clearly discernible gap exists between the letter of the law which, it is surely fair to say, neither withholds rights nor actually grants them, and the practise of the law. Any man contemplating such proceedings obviously needs good informed legal advice. He requires advice not only on his chances of success but on the correct and most hopeful procedure to be adopted according to his individual needs. The legal profession like society in general is not acccustomed to putative fathers taking such action. Consequently, the task of finding a solicitor who is aware of these legal approaches and competent to argue them is not easy. Solicitors, thankfully, cannot advertise, but I am advised that discreet enquiries to the clerk or staff of a court will elicit, not a recommendation, but guidelines. Court staff know who handles what sort of cases and such information can greatly smoothe the path of a father who wishes to bring such an action, particularly when time is often short and speed crucial.

One unmarried father suggested to me that a reform of the present system whereby a father who admitted paternity and who was willing to pay maintenance should be given automatic right of access without the need to invoke complicated legal procedures and without the action being heard in criminal courts seemed practical. The objection to such an idea is obviously one of enforcement. The scheme could work provided an admission of paternity and an automatic willingness to contribute financially to a child's well-being were the order of the day in our society. Sadly, these are not the expectations of our society, nor the instincts of most unmarried fathers. Such a 'voluntary' scheme, therefore, will have to wait on very far-reaching changes in attitudes.

However, much heart can be taken from the increasing number of men and women who are drawing up private agreements concerning their out-of-wedlock children. The advantages of this alternative are enormous. Firstly, they remove any need for appearance by either party in court. Secondly, they are made by the partners *together*, not in contention on either side of a criminal court. Thirdly, the personal needs of the parties, their preferences and individual intentions can be built into the agreement and fourthly, it can be upheld or amended by a court of law should some insuperable difference arise.

The fact that two people who were once close enough, no matter how briefly, to produce a child can sit down and define their willingness to do the best they can for the child is, in itself, a considerable advantage over the formal proceedings of a court. The first thing such an agreement should do is to establish paternity for the child's sake. Even if all that child knows of its father is a name on a legally admitted piece of paper, that is better than the whispered secret so many natural childen have received as their empty inheritance. The chances are, though, that such an agreement will ensure contact between putative father and natural child. It enables these matters to be established without the exchange of money, although many such agreements do allow for the voluntary payment of a sum of money for the child's maintenance. The question of money becomes entirely optional. If the woman needs it and the man can afford it, then at least it can be paid without the reluctance bred of duress. A concerned father can also, under such agreement, arrange for his child to benefit in the event of his death. In short, these agreements are exactly similar to those which unmarried but cohabiting couples have been drawing up for years. Their extension to more casual relationships is to be applauded. Nor is their benefit exclusively directed towards the child. The parents can establish the possibility of conducting a limited but constructive dialogue and avoid the resentful acrimony that invariably attends court proceedings.

While a change in the law seems to me to be essential and urgent, it has clearly got to be made for the benefit of the child first, and the mother as well as the father. A law which gave even rudimentary rights to putative fathers in isolation would be open to possible abuse. Children are already too often used as pawns in some egotistical battle between parents, married as well as unmarried, for anyone to wish to increase that risk. At the same time, while the present system both discourages and depresses putative fathers, no useful purpose would be served by setting them apart from the body of society, or in any way treating them as a special case. The rights and protection now automatically granted to a married father should be simply extended to the unmarried father, with certain additions and exceptions.

The prime object of such a law, in my view, should be the simple and easy establishment of paternity for the child's sake. It seems likely that the development of a foolproof blood test ascertaining paternity is only a matter of time, and that on this question at least, we are only concerned with short-term solutions. When such blood tests are available, I would hope that they become compulsory and a matter of course. If the establishment of paternity remains conditional upon the payment of maintenance, then obviously no true advance will have been made. The fact of paternity should be non-conditional, designed only to give the child knowledge of his father. That knowledge, it seems to me, is his of right and should be available in such a way as to spare him the shame and the sense of rejection which traditionally accompanies its acquisition.

The question of the child's surname seems to me an extremely personal matter. Hopefully, any amendments to the law would be designed to bring unmarried parents together so that such matters could be argued and discussed reasonably between the parties concerned. Socially, there is probably an advantage in the child taking the name of whichever parent he lives with, but it would seem reasonable to give him a choice when he is old enough to choose responsibly.

It is extremely difficult to escape the idea that a putative father should contribute to his natural child's upkeep. To release him entirely from that responsibility would seem to be detrimental to society as well as the mother and child. Its pay-ment can also be detrimental to the man. There may come a time when the weekly or monthly payment of maintenance can inhibit his marrying and establishing a family. That is a state of affairs we have always tolerated partly because the idea of punishment, of making a man pay for his pleasure, is behind our thinking on this subject and partly because of the great difficulty of deciding whether a man should be able to abandon one irregular family to start another. To decide that he may would certainly seem to discriminate against the illegitimate child once again. Similarly, we have tacitly tolerated the evasion of Affilia-tion Orders for these and far less laudable reasons. It is obviously essential to remove once and for all the idea of punishment from laws which apply to unmarried fathers. The defaulter does not benefit his child or the mother, and breaks the law into the bargain.

The question of maintenance, therefore, must surely be optional to the woman, realistically based and subject to review. Certainly women who do not want or require this sort of finan-cial help should not have it forced upon them. Furthermore, it should be obvious that financial support is more necessary at certain times than at others. During pregnancy and when the mother is unable to work because of the child's needs is the time when she most needs help. It would seem logical, there-fore, that the putative father should help when it is most needed, but perhaps not have his family-making potential limited by burdensome financial considerations until the child is sixteen.

In fact, there are grounds for regarding the whole question of paternal maintenance as an academic consideration. Affiliation Orders are seldom, if ever, made for a sum that would actually keep a child, and they are easily evaded by determined men. It seems to me that the obtaining situation is unworkable and that it has got its priorities wrong. We are putting the idea that a man must pay before the welfare of the child. The solution is a simple one, though I can take no credit for it. The National Council for One Parent Families is urging the introduction of a statutory allowance for all children in one parent families as of right. This allowance would not be means tested, and would not therefore preclude the parent of any status and either sex from working. It is a proposal based on the needs and rights of the child of lone parents. The contribution of a father, married or otherwise, would not be discouraged, but the child would be guaranteed an income of sorts. Such an allowance, by being paid to the children of divorcees, widows and widowers, abandoned fathers as well as to unmarried parents, would be a blow against the separatism which still afflicts natural children. In addition it would obviate one of the major hardships experienced by unmarried fathers who wish to assume responsibility for their children.

It is impossible to propose a revision of the present law regarding the maintenance of unmarried mothers without perpetuating that sense of punishment which causes men to default already. Unmarried mothers are not now entitled to personal maintenance. To give them that right would be tantamount to giving them alimony. It would certainly benefit the no doubt deserving woman, but it would effectively limit a man's chances of marrying and leading a normal life. As a result, he would almost certainly default and nobody could pretend that he was not being punished for 'past mistakes'. Nor should we forget that more and more women are refusing to marry the fathers of their natural children. By doing so they are choosing not to be supported by a given man.

In my view, the law should concern itself with the child. The other parties are adult men and women who can be expected to fend for themselves. Obviously, the law must take into consideration the limitations placed on a woman, particularly at certain times, by the presence of a child. It should therefore encourage the father's support and can best do this by giving him some basic rights in the matter.

Human nature being what it is, it seems important that maintenance should be voluntary and that it should entail some rights. There will be a number of men who do not want to pay and who do not want to know. If, however, the payment of maintenance gave him automatic right of agreed, reasonable access and an influence over the child's future and well-being, I believe that more men should accept their responsibility and much of the stigma of illegitimacy would be removed.

The same law would recognize the feasibility of a putative father having custody, care and control of his child. The reversal of traditional roles within marriage has been proved viable. The chances are that such arrangements will increase. The idea of fathers as active, supporting and caring individuals is gradually taking hold in our society. There are even cases where unmarried fathers have assumed total responsibility. As social services improve so will the opportunities for men to bring up their children. As attitudes change, more women are likely to accept this and more men will want the right to choose. At the moment it seems that only when a mother is inadequate or unfit can a man, especially an unmarried man, step into her shoes. There will surely come a time when a significant number of men will unhesitatingly regard those shoes as their own, and for this reason a law which recognizes this possibility, if only in the sense of treating unmarried parents equally with married ones, is essential. The benefits of such revisions to the parties of a common law marriage are obvious. Here, continuing contact between father and child is a distinct possibility and I, at least, do not see how one may continue to distinguish, morally or ethically, between such a man and a divorced father.

The essence of these legal changes should be to bring people together rather than to provide them with legally qualified referees in a court of law. Therefore, it seems indisputable that legislation which takes a positive, non–punitive attitude towards the rights and responsibilities of unmarried parents will operate most effectively in a special Family Court. The proposals of

Judge Jean Graham Hall* show not only that this is a practical idea, but a beneficial one. Such Courts would be locally based and would be Courts of first instance, with right to appeal to the Family Division of the High Court. The proposed Courts would have jurisdiction over Divorce, Annulment, Separation, Maintenance, Guardianship, Custody, Access, Paternity disputes, Affiliation, Adoption and Consent to marry. By bringing all these domestic matters together under one roof, all aspects of a given case could be heard by one bench which would thus have an opportunity to form a rounded picture of the issue. Often, different aspects of the same case could be heard at the same time, which would not only speed matters up but make the whole process much cheaper.

Ideally, of course, such Courts would be housed in separate buildings to ensure complete disassociation from the criminal Courts. Judges and magistrates would be drawn from the ranks of those who already have a wide experience of domestic proceedings and, perhaps more importantly, from those who express a special interest and concern in such matters. It is envisaged that the Family Court would have a very close working relationship with social workers and welfare personnel in an attempt to facilitate its aim of giving priority to the welfare of children, while endeavouring to diminish the bitterness and misery which so often afflict the young victims of domestic disputes.

The Family Court would not be a forbidding place. It would avoid that overwhelming aura of remote power which deters so many and causes others to be tongue-tied. If it were able to enforce suitably amended laws, it might also cease to be the place in which people feel they are making a last ditch and often despairing stand. Indeed, it might be regarded more as a tribunal than as a court of law. Yet it must retain a formality of purpose and conduct. There is much to recommend a central place in which people could gather to thrash out their problems, guided by legal experts, but the risk of abuse is too great to make it practicable. A Family Court would have to hear evidence on oath, would have to be satisfied as to the facts of the case, and would have to make legally binding decisions. It can do all this,

*Jean Graham Hall, *Proposal for a Family Court*, NCOPF, Revised Edition, May, 1973.

however, in an informal atmosphere and without giving that daunting impression that a human problem is sandwiched in between a series of motoring offences and a case of theft.

The family, whether defined by marriage or not, influences us all so greatly and most powerfully at a time when we have virtually no redress against it, that it surely deserves the dignity of its own humane court.

It seems to me inescapable that the granting of greater and more easily established rights to unmarried fathers should be contingent upon their assumption of greater responsibilities. One cannot, however, usefully enforce either rights or responsibilities on those who do not want them. Indeed, I wonder if we are correct in distinguishing, in this instance at least, between rights and responsibilities. A man's right to see his natural child surely entails and implies his responsibility to be concerned with that child. There are always exceptions, of course, and the law must obviously protect the child and the mother from disruptive influences. In the main, however, by granting rights to the unmarried father we are not giving him powers he does not, in the view of many, deserve, but opening a channel of communication between parent and child to their mutual benefit.

To argue against the opening and maintenance of this channel is to assert that by not marrying the man must forego all concern with his child. There is a magic in the act of marrying, apparently, which gives a father the right to influence and to see his child. Avoidance of marriage makes one unfit or unsuitable. It is distressing to realize that we have always put social conformity, some vague idea of a right and morally correct way to live, above the needs of children. We find it difficult to accept that a man might love his child, but not that child's mother. When we grant automatic rights to the unmarried father, we are granting rights to his child. We are encouraging a latent sense of concern and responsibility in men, and giving children at least the possibility of finding their own identity. We are recognizing a bond of love – a bond which is taken for granted only when there is a piece of paper to formalize it, but which we forget it is powerless to excite.

Psychiatrists have shown the importance of contact between children and fathers. That contact is every bit as important to the natural child as to the legitimate. Many, no matter how much we improve the law, will never receive its benefit, but anything society can do to facilitate and encourage it for even a few is essential. Psychiatrists have also shown us the value to children of having one stable parent constantly in their lives. There is no reason why that parent should not be a man, and an unmarried one at that.

New Approaches to the Unmarried Father

The invaluable *Vista Del Mar* researches were conducted over a period of three years, during which time it was initially estimated that a minimum of one hundred unmarried mothers would seek help from the agency per annum. The cases were divided into two groups. In the first group, every effort was made to contact and involve the putative father in casework and in decision-making. Where contact was successfully made, the boy usually received personal counselling designed to consider his feelings, problems etc. not exclusively in relation to the immediate situation. Later on, both boy and girl were brought together, with the benefit of individual counselling behind them, to face the immediate problem of their relationship and their child's future.

In the second group, no attempt was made to reach the father. Group One was therefore considered to be made up of experimental cases, since they represented a new approach. An important and influential factor, which should be borne in mind, was the age and economic dependence of the majority of subjects. 72·4 per cent of the males and 86·1 per cent of the females were under twenty-four. The comparative youth of the subjects, therefore, raises matters which are peculiarly relevant to their situation but which we have not encountered, for example, in the interviews in this book.

The young unmarried father-to-be, particularly since he is likely to be economically dependent, has eventually to turn to his parents. It is from them, often in conjunction with the girl's parents, that he learns of his designated role. Parents, in fact, act as the interpreters and mouthpieces of society. Frequently, they express the general Victorian attitudes that make up the stereotype, but their personal reactions are grossly complicated by shock, concern and a strong sense of subjective failure.

The traditional western system of courtship and marriage, with all its attendant rituals, performs a secondary but useful function in preparing parents to accept the sexual autonomy of their children. Nothing so dramatically indicates the independence of the child as sexual activity. By its very existence this demands a redefinition of the parental role. Parents of unmarried parents-to-be have no time to adjust to the fact of their children's sexuality, nor to their new role. Indeed, when the parents-to-be are very young, the seniors' role is confused. On the one hand the the parents are needed since the chances are that their children cannot cope with the problem unsupported, while at the same time they have to accept the impossibility of exercising complete authority over children who have behaved as sexual adults.

Natural parental concern frequently leads parents to make desperate efforts to protect their children. Pannor, Massarik and Evans noted that this concern frequently generates a great deal of animosity on both sides. Parents sometimes take legal action to protect their sons, and it is common for them to blacken the girl's character and to present her as being solely responsible for the situation. Parents frequently encourage their sons to suggest that the girl had had intercourse with other men which is, under British law at least, still a man's best defence if he wishes to avoid responsibility for the situation.

By proffering such 'advice' parents often reveal their own concerns. Fear that the boy will 'ruin his life' in an unsuitable marriage is often an expression of the mother's wish to retain her son, to deny that she can be so soon displaced by another woman in her son's affections. To this end, the unfortunate girl is invariably 'unworthy' of the boy, at least in his mother's eyes. The girl has only chosen to trap him from among the phantom hordes of her lovers precisely because he is so special and desirable.

Pannor, Massarik and Evans tend to attribute the questioning of paternity, or its outright denial, to fathers rather more than mothers. In this it is possible to glimpse the traditional male reluctance about marriage and the more disturbing cynicism about women as sexual partners. Most fathers, gratified on one level at this proof of their son's virility, but furious at his 'carelessness', are anxious that he should retain his freedom to make his way in the world and, by implication, to enjoy more women. The effect of such counselling, apart from the dishonesty it encourages, is scarcely likely to give the boy a healthy attitude towards marriage, even though that will still be expected of him at a later date.

On the other hand, some parents of unmarried mothers in the *Vista Del Mar* study, particularly when the mothers were teenagers, objected to any attempt to contact and involve the father.

Perhaps this was their first attempt to deny the existence of the father, a denial that enabled them to treat the experiment as fantasy-based and accidental. Or it may have expressed their feelings that the boy had 'already done enough harm' to their daughter – why bring him in now and prolong their agony? In still other instances, the unmarried mother's parents were most anxious to name the father with the motive of heaping punishment upon him, either verbal or legal.*

Pannor, Massarik and Evans also noted a tendency among some parents to avoid any mention of the father and to encourage the girl's hostility towards him when it existed. Comprehensible as these reactions are when we consider the distress, shock and anger inevitably experienced by parents in this situation, they are unrealistic and damaging. To offer the boy an escape hatch by implanting in his mind the idea that a girl who sleeps with him is likely to have slept with others is cynical and does nothing to encourage the boy to face up to his responsibilities. It is an attitude likely to encourage irresponsibility towards women in general. It is the easy solution which may solve the problem in the short term, and to the boy's advantage, but it is based, as are so many of these reactions, on the assumption that all relationships which result in out-of-wedlock pregnancies are casual and exclusively sexual in nature. This is seldom, and certainly not necessarily, true. Were the young couple facing separation or divorce, their parents would make every effort to encourage them to examine their problems and to try to reach an understanding of the relationship. In this situation, however,

*Pannor, Massarik & Evans.

the boy and the girl are positively discouraged from learning from the circumstances they have created. A relationship is thrown away and no attempt is made to capitalize on it or to resolve it in a productive way. Rather there is a desperate attempt to shore up an old and familiar morality: a girl who permits a boy to have intercourse with her is 'no good' and is therefore more fitted to the role of whore than wife.

A similar damaging cynicism is inherent in the attitude of the girl's parents who encourage her hostility. From this she is likely to gain a general mistrust of the male sex. After all, has she not now learned for herself that her parents were right to warn her against masculine venality? The fostering of such hostility is unlikely to assist the girl to form a meaningful relationship later on.

The instinct to exclude the father helps the parents to avoid facing up to the full implications of their daughter's situation. By being an absent focus of blame, the boy facilitates the flow of sympathy towards the girl, who is in obvious need, and who might otherwise be rejected. The idea of punishing the boy for the harm he has done is only a more direct and obvious form of the same tendency. By displacing blame and anger onto one party, the other is able to benefit.

Underlying the attitudes of both sets of parents is the fear that if the couple are encouraged to meet and face the problem together, they risk a resumption of that offensive sexual passion which brought the situation about in the first place. As recently as 1968, it was noted that a number of unmarried mother and baby homes in Great Britain would not allow putative fathers to visit. In exercising such a ban, the home was adopting a quasi-parental attitude which again leads one to suspect an underlying fear of sexuality which partly motivates the instinctual exclusion of the father.

Parents spend considerable effort and emotional energy in urging their children to guide their sex life in some specific direction, often a direction defined by firm religious or ethical structures. They may disapprove of intercourse outside marriage, hoping thereby to set standards that will preserve hallowed values and prevent rash actions – including those that result in pregnancy. Few of the unmarried mothers or fathers in this study appeared to be influenced by parental admonition. Only 2 per cent of the fathers and 1 per cent of the mothers reported feeling any concern about parental disapproval. Either conventional restraints were used little by the parents or, more probably, the admonition of 'don't' simply proved ineffective, at least at a conscious level.*

When such parents discover that their children are about to become out-of-wedlock parents, the outrage to their standards causes them to feel guilty. Somewhere along the line, they have failed to implant these 'hallowed values' and to instil proper respect for them into their children. Few parents pause to consider whether the standards they hold and have apparently failed to impart should not themselves be questioned. Parents are quick to blame themselves when perhaps there is no real failure on their part, only their children's discovery that the standards imparted are irrelevant or unacceptable. The instinct, however, is to reinstate the standards as quickly as possible, to reaffirm the 'right way' and to pretend that it has not been dented by the behaviour of their children. This frequently leads to cynicism among the young who are quick to point out that their parents are primarily concerned to save face with their peers. Pannor, Massarik and Evans discovered that the young have some grounds for this cynicism.

Closely associated with the parents' criticisms of themselves was the question of the extent to which they were concerned about what others might think of them as parents. Approximately 75 per cent of the parents of unmarried fathers were quite concerned about this. In the case of the parents of unmarried mothers, the figure was some-what higher, approximately 82 per cent.†

The difference between these figures, though not great, is explained by the fact that it is easier to conceal unmarried fatherhood. Even so this difference smacks slightly of the old double standard. A girl is ruined by an out-of-wedlock pregnancy, but a boy is not. On the other hand, the surprisingly large number of parents of unmarried fathers who were concerned about the opinions of others does indicate how important this aspect is and, inevitably, it influences parental approaches to the problem.

When all these factors are placed together they tend to produce

*Pannor, Massarik & Evans.
†Pannor, Massarik & Evans.

the same solution. That is, the focussing of care and attention on the unmarried mother and the more or less total exclusion of the father. In fact, the problem is simplified, narrowed down to manageable proportions. The presence and involvement of the father complicates the issue, turns a simple human crisis with clear-cut alternatives into a complex web of human relationships with a past, present and possible future.

The older, economically independent man has an apparently wider range of choices before him. In many ways, it is much easier for him to disappear, to leave the girl to cope as best she may. Certainly there is no need for him to involve his parents. He and his partner, assuming both are older, may find it easier to seek objective help for themselves. Yet, when all is said and done, the older unmarried father still has only the one model against which to measure his behaviour and, perhaps even more than his younger brothers, quite a large section of society, including his peers, are quite ready to endorse his assumption of this stereotyped role.

From the man's point of view, however, the only really significant difference would appear to be that he has the means to offer to pay for and even to arrange an abortion. This solves the problem, at least in the short term and from his point of view. But if the mother-to-be refuses to have an abortion, and marriage is impossible or unwanted, then the male is likely to assume merely financial responsibility. He feels that he has done all that is required of him if he offers money for an abortion, or financial support during pregnancy. The depressing thing is that, in the general view, he is quite right so to think.

The exclusion of the unmarried father and the concentration of attention on the unmarried mother is a viable method of approach only if certain assumptions are made about the people involved in the situation. These assumptions include:
(1) that all such pregnancies are accidental, the result of a casual sexual passion and in all probability the father is a hundred miles away and, in any case, used a false name;
(2) that men who sleep with women before marriage have no sense of responsibility, no concern for their partners and no feelings for their children;
(3) that '. . . unmarried parenthood is an artifact of female

behaviour, disassociated from the acts, attitudes and participation of males.'*

Since even the most cursory research reveals that such
'accidents' are usually avoidable, that most out-of-wedlock
pregnancies result from a definable relationship, and commonsense tells us that since two people are required to cause a
pregnancy the responsibility therefore must be equally shared,
it is obvious that this approach is paradoxical and unrealistic.
More, it contains within it, as I have indicated, at least the seeds
of future damage to both the unwed father and the unwed
mother. To regard the whole problem as an 'accident' incapable
or undeserving of full consideration precludes any serious
attempt to comprehend the situation. In direct contrast to this is
the statement, quoted by Pannor, Massarik and Evans from the
Standards for Services to Unmarried Parents issued by the Child
Welfare League of America.

> The unmarried father, especially the adolescent, should have the
> opportunity for casework help. Social agencies offering counselling
> services, family welfare services, as well as specialised services for
> unmarried parents should *reach out* to the father more than they have
> in the past. They should specify services for unmarried fathers among
> those they offer. At the present time, little professional knowledge is
> available in the literature or from research about the unmarried
> father. Special efforts should be made to work with him and to de-
> velop studies regarding him.

Sadly, this statement, at least as far as the layman is concerned, is likely to produce the reaction 'Why?'. There are many
reasons why, including the proper assumption of responsibilities,
the importance of comprehending and resolving a relationship
that has foundered, concern for the child's future, etc. Of the
important remainder, perhaps the most easily understood and
the most likely to receive widespread sympathetic support is the
benefit to the unmarried mother which results when the man is
actively involved. One of the greatest psychological difficulties
facing her is a sense of rejection. Her feeling of being helplessly
alone is greatly increased when the father of her child, with
whom she has inevitably had some sort of relationship, aban-
dons her. Virginia Wimperis† points out that the physical ten-

*Pannor, NCUMC Lecture.

†Virginia Wimperis, *The Unmarried Mother and Her Child*, Allen & Unwin,
London, 1960.

sion which results from her worry and sense of abandonment may make her actual confinement unnecessarily difficult. When the termination of the relationship has coincided, as it often does, with her announcement of pregnancy, this sense of rejection may well influence her personal reaction to the pregnancy. Resentment of the father may be transferred to the child she is carrying. She may even come to resent the child, whom she blames for the loss of the father. If the father assumes a supportive role during and after pregnancy, many of these unnecessary complications may be avoided.

Every unmarried mother faces a bewildering and daunting series of alternatives. She has to make crucial, far-reaching decisions about her child with which she has got to live for the rest of her life. To place the entire burden of these decisions on the woman is not only unfair but is to deny the very existence of the father and the fact that the couple ever had a meaningful relationship. Only if we accept that unmarried fathers are by nature devoid of the normal concern for their offspring, or that they are totally unsuited to make decisions about the child's future can their deliberate exclusion from the decision-making process be regarded as sensible or desirable.

In the *Vista Del Mar* study, unmarried fathers were encouraged to involve themselves in decision-making, with the following benefit to the mother.

Whenever the unmarried father was willing to stand by the unmarried mother and to share responsibility for her predicament, this proved to be of considerable psychological help to her. Her fear of hostile desertion was frequently dispelled. She could see the father as a person who was not running away but who was concerned, perhaps even frightened – at any rate willing to help. His support of the unmarried mother in her awesome decision regarding the baby was also significant. Our findings showed that when the unmarried father was involved, and when he and the mother could be brought together to discuss what was best for the baby, the mother felt personally reassured and more confident that the final decision was right. Study results also indicated that when the father received agency counselling, he more often supported the mother by approving her decision regarding the baby.*

It is often felt that unmarried fathers can influence their girl

*Pannor, Massarik & Evans.

friends to make an essentially sentimental decision about the baby. Social workers at the National Council for One Parent Families, for instance, state that it is not unusual for unmarried mothers-to-be to decide to keep their babies simply because the men involved have expressed a wish that they should do so, even though they are not prepared to assume a truly supportive long-term role towards the mother and the child. I too have met men who feel, quite unreasonably in my view, that the girl should keep the child when adoption or even abortion would have been a much more satisfactory solution. Girls who heed their boy friends in this matter invariably do so because they entertain hopes of marriage, or at least think that the presence of the child will assure continuing contact with the man. The man's motives are less clearly defined, but it is significant that when expressing this wish he tends to refer to 'his' baby. In other words, the paternal instinct, the sense of having created a child of his own, is often activated by the 'threat' of adoption or abortion, but in a sentimental and impracticable way.

It is this fear that the unmarried father will not be able to put the objective good of the child before his own sentimental sense of paternity that makes many people resist the idea of his involvement. This is a justifiable fear and a danger we should guard against. However, it is a danger considerably lessened by Pannor, Massarik and Evans' approach in which the fathers received counselling as well as the mothers and were thus helped to formulate a realistic view of the primacy of the child's long-term welfare, as well as an accurate assessment of their own commitment to and involvement in the situation.

Involvement on this level also helps the unmarried father. He feels wanted. His sense of failure, of having made a mess of his life, is mitigated by the support he can give. Most important of all he learns about his responsibilities. At the *Vista Del Mar* Child-Care Centre, unmarried fathers were encouraged to see and to hold their babies. Invariably this brought home to them the reality of the situation. The enormous importance of making wise decisions about the future of a new human life became a practical and a meaningful matter. It is important to remember that the vast majority of men, particularly very young ones, can have no real feelings about, or realistic sense of, a child during pregnancy. The whole process, so immediate and real to a woman, is remote from a man. The *Vista Del Mar* project discovered that the best way to reach and involve the unmarried father was through the girl. She is the reality to a man in this position. Emotional appeals to his quasi-paternal sensibilities are likely to be meaningless, but the challenge to understand the relationship, to assist the girl, is a very potent one. Later, the reality of the child and its needs can become an important element in the man's thinking. By such involvement he emerges from the situation with a sense of self-esteem, of having at least been willing to do what he could.

Both unmarried parents, but especially the girls, often entertain entirely unrealistic notions about the relationship. They often feel that marriage is a practical solution, that they could make a success of marriage and be happy if only . . . The involvement of both partners and their counselling frequently enables them to achieve a more realistic understanding of the relationship, to understand why it failed, why it contains no growth potential etc. In some cases, of course, such a programme may create a genuine possibility of a continuing relationship, and even marriage. Needless to say, the traditional exclusion of the putative father precludes any such possibility.

The other crucial element in the argument for increased involvement of the unmarried father is recognition of the fact that he has problems of his own which have at least contributed to his becoming an unwed parent. This, I suspect, is likely to be a particularly unpopular argument on two counts. Firstly, it will seem to many yet another example of the trend to 'go soft' on 'offenders' and secondly because, if the unmarried father is found to have definable psychological problems, it will raise a number of decidedly uncomfortable questions for other people, particularly parents.

The basis for so regarding unmarried fathers is a simple one. While it is undoubtedly true that an overwhelming majority of men seek opportunities to express themselves sexually out of wedlock, the fact remains that only a minority of these become unmarried fathers. It is not therefore unreasonable to ask if there are any discernible reasons why this should be so. The traditional answer is, of course, accident. Some men 'get caught' and some don't. Even the limited amount of systematic research that has been done is sufficient to show that this 'explanation', although convenient, simply will not do. Furthermore, if we regard unmarried fatherhood as an example of anti-social behaviour, in the sense that it constitutes a violation of social norms and standards, we may also ask if this behaviour, like so many other anti-social acts, is not in fact a protest, an attempt to draw attention to a problem rather than mere wantonness or lust.

All research so far seems to indicate that the most common problem faced by the unmarried father and the unmarried mother concerns personal sexual identity. For example:

'For 85 per cent of the cases, male caseworkers concluded that the sexual experience represented an effort by the unmarried father to prove his masculinity. This is further supported by our data, which indicates that 50 per cent of the unmarried fathers in our study lived in homes where fathers were absent or deceased.'*

'The boy who carries out sexual intercourse without contraception is likely to be expressing one or more unconscious attitudes. He may be unsure of his masculinity and feel unconsciously that fathering a child will prove his virility.'†

'Unmarried fathers, like single mothers, cannot be put easily into one category, but a high proportion of them are unstable, immature characters whose own family life has been dispiriting.'‡

In western society, masculine identity is chiefly experienced through sexual performance, while feminine identity is closely equated with motherhood. Both of these activities are expressly forbidden outside marriage, yet in the case of the male, sexual prowess is insisted upon and tacitly encouraged. The absence of a strong identity is often associated with a lack of self-esteem, a tendency to over- or under-estimate personal potential, romanticism and selfishness – all qualities which have been noted by Pannor, Massarik and Evans, among others, as being common among unmarried parents, especially fathers. They conclude that an unmarried father is likely to experience difficulty in adjusting to society and his individual place therein. This difficulty stems not from a lack of social skills or of intellectual abilities, but from a deep-rooted immaturity. A mark of immaturity is a lack of responsibility. Pannor, Massarik and Evans argue

*Pannor, Massarik & Evans.
†*Sex and the College Student*, The Committee on the College Student, Group for the Advancement of Psychiatry, Athenaeum Publishers, New York, 1966.
‡Diana Dewar.

that immaturity is frequently related to identity problems. To summarize, the young unmarried father's behaviour may be seen as an attempt to discover who he is and of what he is capable.

Broken or unhappy home backgrounds often foster poor sexual identity, either through absence of a father-figure, emulation of a bad masculine model, or the simple need to escape the bad home situation by creating a supposedly secure love-relationship for oneself. The frequency with which unmarried fathers come from unsatisfactory home backgrounds is too great to be accidental. This point is further borne out by Diana Dewar's research:

'There is appalling unaniminity to support the observations that the problem of unmarried parenthood is self-generating: an unhappy childhood tends to produce a new generation of irresponsible, if not unmarried parents.'*

Sex for such men is both a panacea and a way of proving that they exist as something more than a pawn in a series of family rows, a surrogate husband for an abandoned mother, or as a creature set apart from others by surroundings and backgrounds. Further, broken or unhappy homes seldom provide sex education on any comprehensive scale. Rather, sex is likely to be regarded as a weapon in the war between mother and father, which breeds irresponsibility and guilt in the child. Psychiatrists and sociologists have confirmed that identity is sometimes realized by father- and motherhood: the baby providing proof positive of virility or fecundity and serving as a much-needed love-object. For the male particularly, the approval and regard of peers is extremely important. Often the only way for a disturbed and unhappy boy to obtain this regard is by feats of daring-sexual-do which all too frequently result in unmarried fatherhood.

Thus it is not surprising that Pannor, Massarik and Evans can say, '. . . unmarried parents are perhaps overly concerned with meeting their own immediate needs. Consideration of the partner or of the consequences of the sexual act was conspicuous by its infrequency.'† Men and women in this position are using sex to prove something about themselves, as an escape route and a means of personal confirmation. Any awareness of the possi-

*Diana Dewar.
†Pannor, Massarik & Evans.

bility of bringing a child into the world is likely to be immediately irrelevant, or subconscious.

This evidence is surely sufficient to establish that unmarried fathers do have problems of their own, and to lay the myth, once and for all, of the men who carelessly scatter their seeds with no thought of the consequences. Such generalizations obviously cannot hold true for every unmarried father, but if only a small proportion are found to have such problems – and I believe that it is more likely to be a majority – that minority alone would be sufficient to encourage the establishment of a social care programme that embodies the idea of 'reaching out' to the men.

To this end, Pannor, Massarik and Evans have evolved eight goals which should be borne in mind when dealing with the unmarried father and which provide a useful summary of the purpose of his involvement.

(1) Standing by the unmarried mother. This lends some dignity to the relationship and is of extreme importance to the mother.

(2) Participating in planning for the child's care and future.

(3) Assuming and meeting financial responsibility.

(4) Examining life-problems revealed by the illegitimate pregnancy.

(5) Recognizing and meeting the responsibilities of marriage and parenthood.

(6) Understanding his attitude towards the child's mother.

(7) Understanding his attitude toward sex and the meaning of sexual relations.

(8) Recognizing his attitude towards fatherhood.*

To this we may add the frequent need for practical sex education and particularly information about contraception.

The practicality of such approaches is proven by the success achieved by Pannor, Massarik and Evans. Nearly 80 per cent of the fathers in their sample study were reached by the agency and of these a majority played an active supporting role. In addition, they also found that under these circumstances the unmarried father is *willing* to make a financial contribution to the mother of his baby. His involvement and concern removes the prevalent sense of punishment. In this as in every other instance, an appeal to the better motives of the unmarried father produced

*Pannor, Massarik & Evans.

comparably better behaviour. Therefore, Pannor, Massarik and Evans conclude:

> However, it is our belief that indeed the father *has* a responsibility, not only to participate in planning for the child's future, but also to examine the personal and social implications of his actions as these affect the unwed mother, himself and – most importantly – the child's destiny. Explorations of alternatives that do not include the unwed father are, at best, halfway approaches to the solution of these problems.*

There is, of course, a danger when urging the adoption of some such programme of seeming to give the unmarried father an inflated importance. This is in some degree unavoidable when arguing against his total exclusion from the problem. Neither view is realistic. Ultimately, of course, the only sensible way of solving the unmarried father's problems and of helping him to accept his responsibilities is alongside those of the mother. The object of the exercise must be to encourage professional and lay persons alike to stop regarding the unwed mother in isolation. Instead, we must regard the situation as the outcome of a probably unsatisfactory relationship which two people have created and now must resolve together.

The tendency of Pannor, Massarik and Evans to define the unmarried father as a deviant is, if not an actual danger, certainly of limited usefulness. Deviant as his behaviour may be in strictly clinical terms, the word is unlikely to encourage the unmarried father to identify himself, or its use to promote his image with the general public. We would do better to regard his behaviour as all too human, and by seeking to comprehend his motives perhaps we may succeed in reducing the number of men who create illegitimate births. Certainly, by encouraging his involvement we can help to provide a better future for the unmarried mother and her child.

The fact that we can now begin to see that unmarried parents are likely to be influenced if not actually created by circumstances beyond their control is a step toward a healthier, more caring society. We know a great deal about and have some sympathy with the problems, distress and acute social disadvantages of the unmarried mother and her child, but we also have to remind ourselves that unmarried fathers are people, too.

*Pannor, Massarik & Evans.

Contraception and the Unmarried Parent

We live in an age of reliable and increasingly available contraceptives. Therefore, we undoubtedly have the means to reduce the number of illegitimate births and of abortions to a minimum. There will always be some unplanned and unwanted pregnancies in and out of wedlock, because of the continuing presence of a socially inadequate group for whom contraception will always be a haphazard mystery; because of those who, as a result of religious beliefs, will not contracept, and because of occasional mechanical failure. If everybody else contracepted regularly and responsibly it would be possible to reduce the number of illegitimate births way below society's toleration threshold and thus free the over-burdened social care agencies to do a more thorough job. In theory, contraception could actually remove the problem of illegitimacy altogether. It is therefore remarkable that no one I have met who is actively engaged in promoting contraception, or who has direct experience of helping the unmarried parent, honestly believes that contraception will ever achieve this solution. In a nutshell it appears that our battery of intra-uterine devices, pills and sheaths are effectively undermined by the very people they are designed to help.

It is this human element which breeds caution among those who are professionally and personally committed to contraceptive education. Everyone has his or her version of the story about the woman who has to search frantically through drawers, ransack cupboards and empty handbags in order to show her health visitor that she is using and is happy with the prescribed diaphragm. 'I know I put it somewhere safe,' is the common cry, but how many eager husbands will contain themselves while this farcical search goes on? It may be safe, but she certainly is not. Such stories do not only concern the flustered working-class wife and mother who, through a combination of embarrassment and ignorance probably never will contracept responsibly. Her much less harassed and supposedly more responsible sisters are plagued with forgetfulness, cannot be bothered, or thought it wasn't necessary because they were 'safe'. The whole situation is reminiscent of that proverbial horse being led to water. You can equip people with contraceptives by the dozen, but you cannot ensure that they will use them.

Everybody concerned with contraceptive education knows that much more could be done if only there were wider outlets for their work. Although progress has been slow, inch by hard-won inch in the face of entrenched resistence, it is accelerating and will probably continue to do so. Some agencies are beginning to think in terms of popularization, to recognize that progress can perhaps best be made by making contraception fashionable. To this end major advertising campaigns have been launched, some of which stress the shared responsibility of contraception. But even if one imagines a vastly improved and extended system of contraceptive availability and information there is still a nagging feeling that counsellors are, to a large extent, beating their heads against a brick wall. They just might manage to contain the flood, but it is difficult to be optimistic about their chances of reducing it.

It is tempting, of course, to criticize both the limitations which have been imposed on contraceptive education and the quality of the work done. While one must recognize that these limitations make it difficult to judge the potential effect of widespread contraceptive education, to carry the criticism any further is to seek convenient scapegoats. We should guard against blaming those working in the field because they face a very complex and deep-seated social resistance which they alone will probably never overcome.

The majority of people still fear contraception as a licence for promiscuity. The traditional association of contraception with family planning means in effect that it has come to be regarded as a practice reserved for married couples only, for, in fact, those who have already obtained a licence to perform sexual intercourse. This was no doubt a right and proper attitude in the early days of contraception, but today it is as anachronistic as the quasi-Victorian stereotypes of the unmarried father. A great many sexual attitudes have changed, particularly among the young. Much as some may dislike this and be genuinely offended by it, we do live in a world where many of the old sanctions about sex no longer operate. Nor can we turn the clock back to those days of preserved virginity and superficial sexlessness. I can see no real choice before us but to face up to this situation. It would be simply humanitarian to utilize more effectively the means at our disposal to prevent at least some of the unwanted pregnancies which blight hopeful lives and simultaneously start others on a disadvantaged and often unhappy path.

I believe that the main reason for this widespread resistance to contraception is the fundamentally anti-sex nature of our society. This is a deeply unpopular view and it is likely to become more so if one examines the implications of it. Contraception is accepted for those who have conformed to society's socio-sexual mode, marriage, and who wish, for whatever reason, to limit their family. The argument, familiar to everyone, is that if we extend, as a matter of course, contraceptive information and means to the young we will automatically encourage them to have sex. This argument might be persuasive if there was any reason to believe the opposite, i.e., that denial of contraceptives prevented people having sex outside marriage. The statistics which often most alarm those who fervently believe in the 'contraception is encouragement' non-argument, overwhelmingly prove the contrary, of course.

Everyone is rightly alarmed at the increase of illegitimate births to school-age girls. This is 'explained' by attacks on eroded moral standards, the pernicious effects of advertising and so-called pornography on television, and even occasionally by the earlier onset of puberty as a direct result of Welfare State molly-coddling. Possibly some of these factors play a part, but it is equally reasonable to assume that this mounting figure is influenced by the fact that it is the very young who have least knowledge of and virtually no access to contraceptive devices. Many older potential unmarried parents may never become such because they possess the maturity and the means to contracept.

Vociferous outbursts of righteous indignation and condemnation greeted newspaper reports of a sixteen year old boy who tried to obtain, in a perfectly legal fashion, birth control pills for his girl friend. This suggests to me that the refusal to give contraceptives to young people has become another (unsuccessful) means of trying to prevent them having sexual intercourse below a certain arbitrary age and outside wedlock. Very few people applauded that young couple for their responsibility. On the contrary, they were said to be irresponsible and immoral.

On this level, of course, contraception is not really the issue at all. It is rather that, for a complex variety of reasons, we want to stop our children having sex because we still believe that sex is generally 'wrong' or 'bad', and certainly not an activity in which the young should indulge. Since history proves that those who wish to prevent the young or even the unmarried expressing themselves sexually are doomed to failure, it could be said that there is really very little to worry about. This is not so because of the damage that can result from illegitimate births both to individuals and to society as a whole. Much of the alarm felt when a new batch of statistics is published showing a rise in illegitimate births and abortions granted to very young girls is based on a sensible recognition that these are the people most unsuited to motherhood and who have most to lose by its premature assumption. Few things are more sad than a fifteen year old girl whose adolescence is blighted by an unwanted child, or traumatized by abortion or adoption. But we allow this state of affairs to continue on a head-in-the-sand principle which conveniently blinds us to the uncomfortable fact that we do regard out-of-wedlock pregnancies as a punishment for bad behaviour. Thus one of the most important and pleasurable aspects of a woman's life, not to mention an innocent, defenceless baby, are regarded as punishments.

Put in these terms, that is dissociated from the sexual act, the majority of people, I think, recognize the immorality, the sheer unkindness of this position. But to prevent this situation arising and to remove the damage it causes requires that parents accept the sexuality and sexual desires of their children. We prefer the unwanted-baby-as-just-punishment syndrome to teaching our children not to damage their own lives and not to create an unwanted life. I do not see how this pernicious rigmarole can be understood except in terms of anti-sex feeling. Everything points to the fact that we want to stop sexual intercourse, not illegitimate births.

Arguments about really comprehensive contraceptive use quickly founder in the realms of fantasy. They do so in the short term because any concerted attempt to make contraceptives available to the young and to encourage their responsible use would meet with similarly concerted opposition which would, I am sure, be effective. However, the time must come. It may come, too, for the science-fiction fantasies of legislation for compulsory contraception. Some people have suggested that an anti-fertility chemical should be added to the water supply of whole nations much as fluoride is today. Quite how one exempts Catholics from the tap, or prevents the species dying out, are questions which scientists and moralists may yet have to face. Today's fiction has a habit of becoming tomorrow's fact and we should not be too ready to dismiss the improbable.

Fantasies about some form of compulsory contraception, chilling though they strike us, are inspired by two alarming facts: overpopulation and human resistance to contraception. Over-population is still a threat to most of the developed nations and should be an effective argument for contraception. It is not harsh, I think, to suggest that before we begin to think about rationing babies among couples who are equipped to be parents and to raise children, we might concentrate on limiting the truly unwanted babies. We must not delude ourselves into thinking that the curtailment of illegitimate births would alone solve the population explosion. It does seem, however, a suitable area in which to make a start, to the benefit not only of an over-crowded society but of unwed parents and their children as well.

Resistance to contraception is obviously central to its failure to help as much as it could and should. In the context of unmarried parenthood failure to contracept when the knowledge and the means are available does seem to support the view that many such pregnancies are not accidental. It seems likely that these couples are, on one level at least, accepting the risk involved and only later, when faced with the reality of an unwanted pregnancy do they attempt to explain the whole thing as an accident. For reasons they almost certainly do not understand – pressure to demonstrate masculinity, desire for a love object, probably as a weapon in some subconscious war with their parents – contraception is dismissed. Again, when intercourse itself is used as a protest or a means of rebelling against parental control, contraception will be avoided since pregnancy is the best way of communicating the protest. This explanation, however, is only applicable to some unmarried parents. The majority, I think, really haven't bothered and partial explanations for this disaffection and failure to consider the full implications of the situation can be found in general social attitudes to contraception and even in the development of the devices themselves.

The fundamental anti-sex feelings which militate against the widespread availability of contraceptives and information about their use influence those who ought to use them most. A person who grows up with an awareness that authority figures such as parents believe that it is wrong for them to have sex are unlikely to contracept because to do so is to admit that they are defying authority, even acting badly. An air of secrecy and of concealment surrounds youthful sexual activity. It really does 'just happen' because, in spite of all the arguments and attempts to make people believe otherwise, it is a natural activity. To suggest that a young and inexperienced person should enter every potential sexual situation armed with contraceptive facilities is to expect a degree of foresight that is exceptional among human beings in general. Furthermore, it demands a level of maturity that is seldom given to the young. Apart from requiring a thoroughly opportunist attitude to life that few people have, it would also argue that the person concerned had reached a conscious decision to live his or her own life in accepted opposition to parents, religious teaching and the views of society in general.

The root of that carelessness of which it is easy to accuse unmarried parents lies in the fact that the majority of them cannot think out a way of life that is contrary to their upbringing until they have discovered an alternative through practical experience. It is necessary for all of us, to a greater or lesser extent, to operate for a while in a no-man's-land between personal freedom and parental control. This is one reason why so many parents of unmarried fathers and mothers are taken completely by surprise. Their children have seemed to adhere to their parents' code because only when they have the experience to back up their defiance and to defend their alternative lifestyle can they admit to being rebels. Tragically, many find themselves in the desperate situation of having created an unwanted pregnancy before that time comes.

Concealment of sexual activity and non-consideration of contraception is reinforced by various social pressures. The ambivalence inherent in the male sexual role is one of these. On the one hand the male is expected and tacitly encouraged to prove himself sexually. To this end, condoms are often purchased and carried as status symbols, or declarations of intent. Certainly during my adolescence, a single Durex in one's wallet was virtually *de rigeur* although few of us had the courage let alone the opportunity to use it. But the young male also knows that girls are taught to resist him, to expect him to make sexual advances which they must reject. Thus the contraceptive becomes an object with which to impress his peers, but it is concealed from girls because he does not wish to appear, in their eyes, as a figure in their received mythology – a boy who is after only one thing.

The boy who produces a condom runs the risk of receiving a rebuff from the girl because she interprets its possession as evidence that he believes her to be 'easy'. His foresight frequently suggests that all his attentiveness and romantic wooing are in fact hollow means to persuade her to have intercourse with him. Alternatively, the girl might read his contraceptive foresight as meaning that he has had a succession of sexual encounters and therefore that she does not occupy a unique place in his affections.

In American studies it is quite common to hear of boys who do not contracept because they really care about the girl concerned. The implication here is that a boy only contracepts with a girl for whom he feels nothing but desire, who is therefore deemed to be promiscuous and a possible source of venereal infection. Whether this is actually intended as a demonstration of commitment to the loved girl – 'If you get pregnant, I will stand by you' – or is lingering evidence that prophylactic sheaths were originally intended to afford protection against venereal disease, I do not know. Both ideas are probably at work, but whatever the explanation these findings underline the fact that contraception is associated in many young minds with a lack of respect and feeling for the partner.

This broadly social dilemma surrounding contraception is not limited to boys. It is very difficult for a young girl to obtain contraceptives. Because female contraceptive devices have to be prescribed or fitted, their acquisition demands a very sophisticated degree of personal commitment and courage. Most young women only reach this point once a stable relationship has been achieved. Women, in fact, tend to contracept for one man. It is still rare for a girl to contracept on the assumption that she will be sleeping with somebody sooner or later. To do so is to bring herself into conflict with the pressure placed on her and her personal desire to be a nice respectable girl. In order to contracept at all she has to undo years of teaching and overcome her ignorance of such things. Indeed, to contracept can even bring her into conflict with men, many of whom feel that a girl who announces that she has taken proper precautions is little better than a whore. Her precaution indicates a sexual willingness which runs counter to the ideas about women they have inherited from their parents. They feel that a girl who contracepts outside a firm relationship must be 'anybody's' and tend to treat her accordingly.

Intra-uterine devices, even if available, are not practical for the young girl. Many young women feel repugnance at the idea of fitting a diaphragm, for example, and to do so is, sometimes, impractical until they have had some sexual experience, by which time it may already be too late. Oral contraceptives are, in fact, the only realistic solution for the young woman and these, inevitably, are the most difficult to obtain.

Place all these conflicting attitudes together and a situation is created in which contraception cannot figure because it represents a threat to personal relationships and to self-esteem.

The fact that contraception is, in general, regarded as having relevance only within marriage also militates against its practice among potential unmarried parents. Pannor, Massarik and Evans, for example, report that a number of unmarried fathers declared that they would contracept after marrying but had never seriously considered doing so in pre-marital sexual situa-

F

tions. This extraordinary attitude can only explained by imperfect understandings about contraception, coupled with an inability to face up to the possible consequences of the act. Undoubtedly, what little many young people learn about contraception is within the context of family planning. This is especially true for girls. As such it means little to them because the idea of their marrying and having a family is something way on in the future. Contraception is therefore irrelevant to their situation because they are not planning a family, simply having sex. This regrettable state of affairs is brought about by our insistence on restricting contraceptive information to the marriage situation. Just as children and even many adolescents believe that babies only occur to married couples, so contraception has no discernible point of connection with their sexual behaviour.

All these attitudes to contraception indicate that the subject has become unprofitably associated with the whole mythology of sex in the minds of the young rather than being seen as a practical means of preventing conception. Certainly the little I learned about contraceptives as a youth was within the context of sexual performance. Contraception was, in fact, just one element in the whole amorphous mass of sexually titillating information which excited and embarrassed. The practical aspects of contraceptives did not impinge. This again is a failure of education. By regarding contraceptive information as something unsuitable for children and adolescents we assure that it is not taken seriously. It becomes instead a subject for dirty jokes, part of the giggle-inspiring speculation about sex.

This lack of information and the confused attitudes it breeds gives rise to an alternative mythology which frequently 'justifies' the failure to contracept. Girls cannot conceive until they are married, or until they have had a long period of sexual experience. Conception is prevented if intercourse is performed standing up. Boys aren't fertile until they're twenty-one, or married, or if they masturbate. *Coitus interruptus* is a reliable method of contraception. Girls automatically undergo a virtually unlimited 'safe' period. All of these myths are regularly trotted out as reasons why the couple did not need to contracept. The credence they are given indicates a suppressed knowledge of the risk taken. They are sops with which people reassure themselves immediately and seek to justify themselves in the long term.

They apparently fill a gap left by the lack of real contraception knowledge.

These are some of the most common ways in which general attitudes to contraception filter down to potential unmarried parents and become twisted and confused with social concepts of niceness, goodness, respectability and commitment to relationships. There are, however, a number of practical aspects of contraception which must be considered in tandem with these received and misinterpreted ideas.

We should never overlook the question of ignorance. It is fashionable now for parents to say, 'Kids these days know more at fifteen than I knew at twenty-five.' This may be true, but it does not mean that they know everything or even enough. Some young people really do not gain any realistic knowledge about contraception. Often they only hear about it in the context of the dirty joke, or as something 'naughty' mummy and daddy keep in a bedside drawer. Embarrassment and a fear of being seen to be ignorant among apparently more worldly-wise peers often leaves them in more or less total ignorance. This can persist right into adult life, and even be confused with scraps of information which may give the appearance of knowledge where none in fact exists.

One social worker who has done a great deal of work with unmarried fathers pointed out the necessity of really probing a young man's sexual and contraceptive knowledge before it is possible to be sure that he actually knows anything at all. There are problems of nomenclature and linguistics – even today it is possible to meet young people for whom intercourse means a kiss and a cuddle. I suspect, although I have no evidence to support it, that the embarrassment which still surrounds contraception often leads researchers to accept bald statements such as 'Oh yes, I know all about contraception' at their face value. It is very easily done. One unmarried father to whom I talked assured me that he not only knew about contraception but that he had made a study of the various methods. Since such claims are rare and he was a man in his mid-twenties, I believed his statement. Later in the conversation he informed me that, now that he realized the importance of reliable contraception he always used the diaphragm! Whether this was a linguistic confusion or whether he had acquired an all purpose diaphragm which he enjoined various girls to wear I was never able to discover. Once challenged even the avowedly knowledgeable tend to retreat into embarrassed silence.

Embarrassment is underestimated as a factor in the failure to contracept. It is very difficult for a boy to go into a shop and ask for a packet of contraceptives. Many shopkeepers set themselves up as moral judges and refuse to sell them to would-be purchasers because they are, in their opinion, too young. Refusals of this kind are usually accompanied by a moral homily which breeds resentment and unnecessary shame. If the youth is foolhardy enough to visit a local barber shop where he is known he often meets with threats of having his request reported to his father. Alternatively, the purchase may be accompanied by invidious remarks about 'good times ahead' and 'lucky young dogs' which offend and embarrass as well as reinforce the masculine myth of a united male sex taking what it wants from the female. The purchase of contraceptives is also a public avowal of intention which runs contary to adolescent feelings about sex. We are taught to keep our sex lives to ourselves and this secrecy is augmented among the young who know that they are doing wrong in their parents' eyes. This makes the purchase of condoms even more traumatic. No wonder, therefore that contraceptive dispensing machines in pub lavatories are so popular, and how typical of our attitude that they are common only in places officially barred to those under eighteen.

Girls, of course, cannot obtain reliable contraceptives over the counter and the rare girl who does attempt to obtain the pill from her family doctor usually leaves herself open to similar damaging criticism and reactions. There are agencies now which will cater for the needs of young women but to visit one demands a maturity which very few young girls possess even if they happen to know about the service.

Availability alone means that the boy is more likely to contracept than the girl. As I have attempted to explain, the intention to do so is often frustrated by the girl's reactions or by the boy's fear that to do so will impair the immediate relationship. Then again, this balance in the boy's 'favour' should not make us cynical about the many situations in which sexual intercourse becomes a possibility when the boy is contraceptively unprepared.

A boy who maintains that he would have contracepted had he known that he was going to have sexual relations, or who just did not happen to have one with him is not always making empty excuses. He may actually attempt to do the next best thing and to withdraw at the crucial moment. To expect him to abstain or to be expert at *coitus interruptus* (which is, in any case, not a contraceptive method at all) is to forget the urgency of youthful desire and the lack of experience which accompanies it. Responsible use of contraceptives does demand a degree of preparation and commitment which is often impossible in pre-marital sexual situations. Most such encounters occur in far from ideal settings and unexpectedly. The back seat of a motor-car, during a party, or in some semi-public place where fear of interruption adds more urgency to the proceedings are all factors which work against the use of contraceptives even when they are available. It is easy to read these failures as excuses, to say that both partners should pause to think about the possible consequences, but to do so is to speak with the voice of experience and the benefit of hindsight. It also ignores the fact that the majority of sex education does nothing to inculcate any such responsible attitude. Consequently, the idea that pregnancy can result from their behaviour is very remote from most young people, a situation which incomplete sex and contraceptive education does nothing to ameliorate.

If there is one factor which influences the non-use of contraceptives by young potential unmarried parents more than any other it is, to my mind, the nature of the most readily available method. This is something which men, on the whole, are very loth to admit, again because of the implications. A contemporary of mine described the experience of making love while wearing a condom as being 'like sucking a toffee with the paper on'. To express this view is to admit that one is indeed a man concerned with his own pleasure. Yet I have never heard a defence of the condom. Everyone agrees that it limits pleasurable sensations and this is no doubt why it is so often avoided.

It is entirely in keeping with the anti-sex attitude which I have described as underlying all contraceptive information that the one relatively cheap and easily available method is both the least pleasant to use and, in the opinion of experts, one of the least safe. Originally, the sheath was intended as a protection against venereal disease. Its contraceptive efficacy was, in fact, a secondary consideration but, at the risk of sounding cynical, I suspect that the fact that it does limit pleasure is one reason why its availability is acceptable to society at large. Perhaps somebody somewhere hoped that it would prove to be deterrent to sexual activity when in fact it has been largely abandoned because of its negative effects on pleasure.

Furthermore, the thinking behind the development of the condom was essentially sexist. Men had to be protected from women as the purveyors of disease – a one-sided and incomplete argument if ever I heard one. Subsequent developments and improvements have continued this sexist trend, with disastrous effects on the whole state of contraceptive use and, to a lesser extent, on the relationship between the sexes. The reliable methods are those which do not curtail physical sensations and which are designed exclusively for female use. Underlying these developments is an honest recognition that women have most to lose by becoming pregnant but the effect is to further dissociate men from what is an undeniable partnership. Then again, intra-uterine devices and oral contraceptives can be effectively limited as to availability by the necessity to fit and to prescribe accurately. In view of this it is very difficult to argue against men, and particularly unmarried fathers, who say that it is the woman's responsibility, not theirs, to contracept. Inevitably this situation reinforces the model of the unmarried father. 'Well,' they say, she went and got herself pregnant. She ought to have done something about it.'

Periodically, we hear vague reports about a male contraceptive pill, but where is it? Certainly the programme of research, as reported by the media, strikes one as less than enthusiastic. It will be argued, of course, that even if a reliable and properly tested oral contraceptive for men is developed there is no reason to believe that men will use it regularly. Certainly there are no grounds to think that men are any less forgetful or careless than women. It is difficult to imagine that many parents would agree to ensure that their teenage sons took their daily contraceptive pill at breakfast each day. However, there is some cause for optimism about the use of a male pill. It, too, could become a peer-oriented status symbol but without the problem of usage already discussed with the sheath. Also, it could be promoted in such a way as to appeal to the already current ideas of male responsibility. To assume certain responsibilities is very much a part of the defined male role, and there is no reason why contraceptive responsibility should not be added to this cannon. It would require that boys be made a much greater focus of contraceptive education than they are at present, but that is in any case desirable. Since it is much more likely that science will develop such a contraceptive than it is that society will radically redefine its image and expectations of the male sex, there is little alternative but to utilize and extend the existing masculine model in this positive way.

Agencies concerned to promote contraception are aware of the need to make it a shared activity, even within marriage. This is difficult to do with existing methods but essential if a national contraceptive habit is to be formed. Any pleas for a male oral contraceptive, therefore, should not preclude further refinement of female methods. A joint solution would be ideal. At the moment, women believe that it is the man's responsibility, while men, basing their views on the greater effectiveness and non-interference with pleasure of female contraceptives, tend to place the burden on women. Both sexes, especially when young, suffer from the embarrassment which still surrounds the topic and therefore seldom discuss it responsibly. 'I thought she'd taken care of it.' 'I thought he'd see to that.' The result is an unwanted pregnancy. Because of our neglect of male contraceptive methods I believe we encourage irresponsibility in men, with the result that many become unmarried fathers. Why should they deny themselves the prime impulse to sexual intercourse – pleasure? But why should women, for whom contraception is often quite difficult, assume sole responsibility? The contraceptive situation is yet another link in a chain of blame and dispute between the sexes which fosters lack of respect and care for which, of course, unmarried parents, especially fathers, are fiercely criticized.

The hysterical publicity given to improved and new methods of female contraception also influence individual male attitudes. Because they read half-baked, alarmist stories in the popular press, many young potential unmarried fathers believe that every girl today is on the pill, or fitted with an intra-uterine device. 'I just assumed that she would be taking care of it.' The media stress the efficiency of methods, pronounce upon their unlikely and unfounded effects on morals but do not point out that most young women have very little chance of obtaining contraceptives. One young man said, 'If I meet a girl who is willing to sleep with me, I just take it for granted that she's on the pill.' Not surprisingly, he is an unmarried father.

The American research conducted by Pannor, Massarik and Evans reflects similar patterns. Almost fifty per cent of the unmarried fathers interviewed for that study said that they did not like contraceptives and therefore did not use them. These enquiries found that lack of knowledge about contraception was not a significant factor in the failure to practise and it is further reported that 'a vast majority did not feel that difficulty in *obtaining* contraceptives was a factor in limiting their use.'* Obviously, these findings relate to the male contraceptive and therefore confirm my own views. The publication of The Committee on the College Student, Group for the Advancement of Psychiatry, *Sex and the College Student*, places ignorance of the relevant facts as an important influence but adds that those 'familiar with the information fail to act in accordance with it for reasons based in unconscious motivation and conflict'.

In other words, psychiatric opinion favours the interpretation that failure to contracept when possible indicates a desire to cause a pregnancy. While it would be foolish to discount the importance of this interpretation it should never be used as a blanket generalization that smugly explains each and every out-of-wedlock pregnancy. In summing up on the topic, Pannor, Massarik and Evans lay great stress on the importance of contraceptive users possessing 'maturity and the psychological authority required for successful usage.'† They add, 'Contraception requires time, privacy, assurance and conscious recognition of the sexual act and its consequences. It also requires ability to deal with reality, to plan ahead and to have a conscious recognition of the needs and wants of others.'‡

In the present social climate it is pointless to blame all but a few illegitimate births on a conscious failure on the part of unmarried parents to contracept. For a majority, and particu-

*Pannor, Massarik & Evans.
†Pannor, Massarik & Evans.
‡Pannor, Massarik & Evans.

have to reassess the whole philosophy behind contraception. It is not something designed exclusively for women's protection, primarily within marriage, but something which centrally concerns both men and women, irrespective of marital status, as equal partners.

In addition, contraceptive information will have to be provided naturally and by people who can reach the young without experiencing or giving embarrassment. Perhaps, as is so often the case, we would have to educate parents first, but various youth organizations, schools and colleges could also provide proper contraceptive counselling on a widespread and effective scale. Such education will not be useful, however, if it is an option for the curious and the bold. It has got to reach everyone as a natural part of education and the maturation process. In my own experience and that of other parents who attempt to assume responsibility for educating their children sexually, the idea that one damages or inhibits a child by imparting such information too soon is nonsense. The information is simply irrelevant if given too soon and will have to be repeated at opportune moments until it becomes comprehensible. Even if the child does not immediately understand, the subject is, as it were, in the air and therefore does not come as a complete shock at puberty. Adolescents turn in on themselves and cannot suddenly communicate with their parents on a topic which is preoccupying them but which has previously been unmentionable. It is important to establish an atmosphere conducive to such communication long before the facts can have much meaning to the children. Similarly, mass sex education must not be frustrated by arbitrary concepts of readiness. The age at which people are generally considered to be ready is, in any case, usually much too late. Embarrassment and fear of encouraging sexual activity is all that really prevents us giving the right information as it is required. That embarrassment communicates itself to the people in need of guidance and instruction. It inhibits their questions and leaves them with no alternative but to experiment in an attempt to discover the answers for themselves. Too often those experiments result in out-of-wedlock pregnancies.

No arguments for better contraceptive education and wider availability can persuade unless our ingrained attitudes to sex itself are greatly revised. We have found threats and punishments as a means of curbing sexual curiosity to be entirely ineffective. At best they cause damage to individuals. To offer contraception to the young certainly demands that we accept their sexuality and their right to express it, but it is not a defeatist solution. It creates an opportunity for those who care to make an appeal to reason and to give that over-worked concept 'responsibility' a new and relevant lease of life. People young and old do like to be responsible but they need to be shown how, in a positive not a negative way, and they need to be given the tools with which to act responsibly. Contraception will probably never eradicate illegitimacy – everyone is agreed about that – but it can prevent a large number of illegitimate births and the heartaches which accompany them. Prevention is always better than cure, especially if you are a bastard in a society which does little and cares less.

The Unconcerned Majority

In 1971, 65,678 illegitimate births were recorded in England and Wales. As far as it is possible to tell some 56,000 women kept their babies. We know for certain that of these possible 56,000 women 7,968 applied to the Courts for Affiliation Orders against alleged putative fathers. 7,053 of these applications were granted. These figures do not tell us to what extent, beyond being legally responsible for some financial aid, these 7,053 recipients of Affiliation Orders are involved with their children. Of the remainder, an estimated 48,947 fathers, some will have reached private agreements, some will be cohabiting and playing a full parental role, but no matter how generous our estimates of those numbers, it is obvious that a great many unmarried fathers are not at all involved, presumably from choice. Is there, then, any point in reaching out to such men, and do we have the right?

There is a case to be made for these men, especially when non-involvement is the result of a conscious decision. It is true that such decisions are likely to be rationalized after the event. The impulse to extricate oneself from an immediate untenable situation is nearly always more powerful than the wish to reach a balanced, considered decision. Subsequent rationalizations, however, are not necessarily invalid. It is important that our rightful concern for the blameless and dependent child should not become a pious excuse to sacrifice the needs and happiness of adults. It would be a stern Solomon indeed who could judge between the individual long-term needs of an unmarried father, an unmarried mother and an illegitimate child. The moment one tries to weigh the one against the other, one runs the risk of deciding that a man, because of his supposed greater sense of responsibility, shall live in recompense for past mistakes. Or that a woman shall live on the breadline because of her previous wantonness. In short, arguments along these lines become tainted with some idea of punishments which I at least find unacceptable, especially since the punishment is invariably visited on the child as well as the parents.

The supposedly unpleasant fact of the matter is that a man can thoroughly enjoy sexual intercourse with a woman for whom he has no other feelings. Obviously one wishes that he would therefore ensure, as far as possible, that pregnancy does not result from such encounters. If he does not, however, it is difficult to advocate his full involvement with his child. Without some more realistic basis for communication with the woman, the chance of his forming a truly worthwhile relationship with his child are slight. Probably the mother will resent him and his contact may interfere with her prospects of forming a more stable relationship. Such contact is likely to peter out when he forms another relationship and possibly fathers other children. There can be little doubt that, in many situations, the child is likely to be better off with one parent and the prospect of a step-parent than a sort of enforced, temporary and intermittent paternal concern. In short, it is neither fair nor accurate to assume that every unmarried father who absents himself is only thinking of himself. In the long run, the rule of thumb approach – if you can't help, don't interfere – may not be such a bad one.

Must we assume, therefore, that such men are deficient in those paternal emotions which influence the majority of my interviewees? I think not. To absent oneself is not to be deficient in feelings, but does suggest a certain ability to stifle such feelings. This is comparatively easy for a man, especially if he never has any personal knowledge of the living child. Pregnancy remains a mystery from which it is easy for a man to detach himself. The unseen foetus in the womb of a woman who has become a nuisance, an embarrassment, or even an object of repugnance, is not likely to awaken deep paternal feelings. I am certain that such feelings can be awakened in a positive and constructive manner, but whether it is wise to do so, as a matter of course, is debatable.

To foster paternal affections which can have no ultimate fulfilment seems to be analogous to that extraordinary practice of insisting that an unmarried mother nurse her child for a period before adoption. During that period maternal bonds are realized which make the final parting that much more traumatic, when they do not persuade the girl to change her mind altogether. It is difficult not to suspect a quasi-moral rigidity in this, a feeling that the mother *should* keep her child, even though she has decided otherwise.

Men are fortunate that they are not placed in a comparable position, and it would be irresponsible to advocate some automatic prodding of paternal emotions if these are likely to be eventually frustrated. For the majority of unmarried fathers comprehensive involvement is likely to be unwanted and unproductive. Therefore, any attempt to encourage the father's participation must have very clear and limited ends. It should enable him to come to terms with the situation he has in part created. It should provide an opportunity for him to help the woman financially during pregnancy and for as long afterwards as is necessary and possible. Above all, the sum paid should be a realistic one. He should be able to help and to support in the decision-making.

The establishment of these approaches would obviously benefit the committed father. Acceptance of the idea of paternal participation in this limited sense should create the machinery for greater involvement in those cases where this is desired and practical. None of the parties will benefit from a horde of fathers urgently trying to wrest their babies from mothers, or frustrating plans when they have no means of housing or supporting the child. There should rather be a balance between exclusion and long-term involvement and, no matter how our sympathies are aroused and may urge us, we should not seek to deprive a man of his freedom to disassociate himself if that is what he wishes. We can and should ask much more of him, but not seek to make this an enforceable demand, or in any way attempt to invoke the law against fathers beyond the sort of Affiliation Proceedings we now have. These could be improved and stengthened, but not extended.

The object should in fact be to open as many doors as possible. At the moment, we can point to a small body of men who are frustrated and distressed by the lack of opportunities to express their unmarried paternal concerns. By smoothing the paths of men who have already committed themselves, we can reasonably hope that more men will make that commitment. For that probable majority who never will, we can at least offer some help, some measure of understanding, while giving their children the right to a surname and an identity. There are, obviously, degrees of involvement. It is as foolish to imagine that we can automatically turn every unmarried father into a loving, concerned parent as it is to dismiss them all as selfish, irresponsible men for whom nobody should have any time. Ultimately, each individual man will have to make his own decision about involvement, will have to assess honestly how far *he* can go, what *he* really feels. It is up to society to give him the opportunity and to make sure that he is aware of the alternatives. Until we establish a pattern of reaching out, of trying to involve the unmarried father as a matter of course, we cannot know how many will respond, or to what degree. By establishing some such general pattern of approach we can accommodate the committed father and stop treating him as an impractical, sentimental creature who is, first and foremost, an administrative nuisance.

Last Words

How much longer, I wonder, can society continue to regard illegitimacy as an exceptional fact to be treated in isolation? Already there are an increasing number of men and women who live together and raise children without the blessing of the church or a civil marriage. These children, although technically illegitimate, are seldom considered as part of the problem because they are cared for within a family situation and because they escape the more dangerous aspects of stigmatization. The appearance of marriage is apparently sufficient for society to accept them.

Similarly, more and more women are refusing to commit themselves publically and legally to one man while insisting on their right to bear and raise children. Since such women usually have adequate financial support, housing etc., society does not seem particularly disturbed by the illegitimacy of their children. Surely this sort of acceptance can be extended to all the other illegitimate children, their mothers and fathers.

Not so many years ago, on a radio programme, a panel of pundits were asked to consider whether the abolition of marriage might not be justified on the grounds that it would remove the stigma of bastardy. To a man, the panel resisted the idea. So great was their shock reaction to this apparent threat to the *status quo* that they refused to accept that such a drastic measure would remove the idea of illegitimacy at all. Thus they ignored, or did not see, the real point of the question – that illegitimacy is an artificial, socially created phenomenon. After all, the bastard is frequently referred to, quite accurately, as a natural child. It is strange that a child may be natural yet not lawful, genuine or real as, among other things, the *Oxford English Dictionary* defines 'legitimate'.

It is similarly strange that any suggestion that we might abolish marriage is (rightly) attacked on the grounds that to do so would be to deny people a basic human freedom, yet there is no comparable outcry against enforcing marriage. Of course there is no law in the land that says one must marry, but society expects it and still takes a broadly condemnatory view of those who do not conform and their children. It seems to me that we must begin to consider the possibility of regarding marriage as an alternative rather than as a rule. Furthermore, the present problems posed by illegitimacy must be regarded in this broad context. The problems are of immediate concern and cause such real distress that they must be tackled directly and sympathetically, but long-term planning should not make the mistake of assuming that attitudes will not change. Certainly we shall never succeed in preventing or eliminating the natural child, but we can encourage and work towards a society in which he is regarded as a whole and equal person; a society in which his parents are not subjected to blanket moral judgements which are suspect in themselves and frequently irrelevant to the situation.

I am convinced that we must follow the lead given by National Council and see the natural child and his parent of whichever sex, as a One Parent Family. Socially, there must be no distinction between the natural child and the offspring of divorced parents, for example. Economically, there is bound to be a difference, and a crucial one at that.

The whole question of finance for the unmarried mother and her child is a difficult one. Society resents the idea of a woman and child – the result of a man's 'selfish pleasure' – being a so-called burden on the State. Payments under Affiliation Orders are seldom large enough to keep a child. In order to make such payments realistic we would have to make them a recognized instrument of punishment directed at the man. Even those who think that this would be no bad thing will accept, I think, that men would simply default, as so many do now when much smaller sums are involved. The idea of a statutory allowance to all children in single parent families is perhaps a compromise but one which is likely to be acceptable. It would have to be supplemented, hopefully by the man, probably by the State, during the child's infancy. It would have to be backed up by many, many more day-care centres, crèches etc. all operating on realistic hours and at no charge to the unmarried parent.

Any such payments and services must, of course, be automatically available to the single father who is caring for his child, be he separated, divorced, widowered or unmarried. Before we reach this point, however, we shall have to change much more basic and deep-rooted attitudes which militate against all lone fathers. A man who wishes to stay home and care for his child is likely to encounter a peculiarly nasty piece of bureaucratic double-think. I have heard social workers admit that their code of practice requires them to encourage the lone male parent to work. A man's place is in the factory or the office, not the home. A man who chooses domesticity and total daily care for his child is regarded as work-shy, perhaps a malingerer. Often, he is advised to get or keep a job in order to support the child, only to be told that the job disqualifies him from looking after the child. Children have been taken into care as a result of this double-dealing, even though the father wanted to keep them together in a stable home. No one would pretend that a single woman finds it easy to get help, but at least she is expected to care for her child and is regarded as a normal person. Men are not only prevented from caring for their children, they are frequently made to feel abnormal for even trying to do so.

It is quite within our power to provide the unmarried parent and his or her child with a secure and reasonably comfortable place within society. To do so, however, we will have to learn to accept them as ordinary men and women, with ordinary babies and children. We will have to accept their right to a decent life, equal opportunities instead of clinging on to outraged moral standards and pious theories about the natural child being necessarily disadvantaged.

Even thirty years ago the idea that an unmarried man should publically own and express concern for his child, let alone seek to raise it himself, was unthinkable. There is no single explanation for this startling change. Economics have played a part, as has the development of the Welfare State. It is now actually possible, though by no stretch of the imagination easy, for a man to stay at home and care for a child or, like Luke, to combine study with child-raising. Our vastly increased knowledge of the early needs and problems of children has gained familiarity and has significantly altered our attitude to children. It is not that we are necessarily more concerned, but rather that we are concerned in a different way. Increased leisure has undoubtedly enabled men to see more of and get more enjoyment from their children. That contact has created a lively awareness of the problems and needs of children which is backed up by actual knowledge. Men have suddenly been placed in a situation in which it is possible for them to compare the actuality of their children's experience with the memories, good and bad, of their own childhood. When I was a child, parents were determined that their children should have something better than they had. Today, parents want what is best for the child. The difference is a subtle one, but it reflects something of our new awareness of children which has probably had a greater impact on men than women simply because it is entirely new to them.

Women, of course, have played an enormous part in the development of what might be termed this new paternal conciousness. The need and wish of more mothers to work has, again, often exposed the father to greater contact with his children. Once a father returned home in time to kiss his pyjamaed offspring good night. Now he is more likely to have to bath and entertain them while a working wife and mother prepares supper or catches up on the ironing. Increased paternal contact and involvement may have begun out of necessity but women, again with the backing of psychology, have been quick to demand paternal contact with children, partly out of a perfectly reasonable wish to share the burden of responsibility, and partly because they know that such contact is essential to the well-being of the child. Besides, men enjoy it. It seems to me significant that some of the most responsible unmarried fathers are very young and may therefore be considered representatives of a generation which is used to the idea that father changes a nappy and picks up toys as a matter of course. The forbidding paterfamilias has been humanized into an available, practically involved man. This process has undoubtedly done much to alter men's expectations of fatherhood.

Similarly, men's domestic competence has increased with

practice, simply because it has been freed from sniggering criticism. A very short time ago a man in an apron, wielding a dishmop, was a figure of postcard fun. Now, if he is not known to participate in the domestic chores, he is likely to be criticized as a chauvinist. With practice he has discovered his abilities as cook and bottlewasher, and with no implied threat to his masculinity.

In fact, the whole view of the masculine role is being subtly eroded. It is really amazing to think that we live in an age in which a great many young men have become 'heroes' by refusing to fight in Vietnam. Not so long ago they would have been handed the emasculating white feathers of tradition.

Even so, we still live in a society in which virility is closely linked to identity. The barren woman inspires genuine pity, but the impotent man is a cruel joke, made to feel that he has 'failed' as a member of his sex. I have already indicated how the exercise of virility, the pressures upon men to prove their sexuality, can contribute to the fact and the resulting confusion of unmarried parenthood. These pressures still exist and continue to take their toll. Some men, however, seem to be turning this particular double standard back on society. Having proved their virility or, more accurately, having expressed their sexual urge, they refuse to hang their heads in shame and disappear. They have fathered a child and are proud of doing so. Their pride is in that child, not the fact of its illegitimacy. I have found no evidence at all of pride in having gone against the dictates and morals of society. More often the fact of illegitimacy is regretted but it breeds a determination not to let this affect the child adversely. Occasionally, the expectations of society have been so whole-heartedly rejected as to entirely rule out any question of bravura pride in transgression.

All of these factors, in so far as they contribute to a general climate of feeling and opinion, help to make it possible for men to assume an unprecedented degree of parental responsibility outside wedlock. However, the actual routes to such decisions seem to me to be rather more simple. Faced with a child, *his* child, at risk for whatever reason, the man tends to act, to assume responsibility because the alternatives seem to him wrong, or inadequate, or undesirable. Such decisions, with all their immensely far-reaching complications, obviously cannot be taken without genuine feelings for the child, but these are not the sole, nor indeed the prime reason for the decision. This, I think, is a fair if simple summing up of Luke's case, for example. In other cases, of which Bill and Andrew in their different respective ways would be examples, the impulse to involvement is essentially emotional. Their feelings for their children are so strong, so instinctive, that separation from them is unthinkable. These men become militants, prepared to fight for their rights, but they are sufficiently realistic about themselves and their situation to realize that the assumption of total responsibility is simply impractical. A few years ago such a man would either have had to marry the mother, or bear as best he could the distress separation must cause. Today, these men demand greater rights, or perhaps one should say, the simple right to be a loving father.

All of us are so conditioned by our own experience, by centuries of habit and the time in which we live that we tend to assume that two parents are always and necessarily better than one. There is much evidence to support this, and a great deal to indicate the disadvantages of the single parent family unit. But there are chinks in the wall of certainty to which, I sometimes suspect, we are blinded by emotion and fear of change. These chinks appear as the widespread acceptance that one reasonably contented parent is better for the child than two quarelling, tense and unhappy ones. And everybody with experience of the single parent family can point to success stories. It is also beginning to be admitted that some children of the conventional and supposedly desirable family unit are damaged and disadvantaged in ways which are remarkably similar to those for so long considered the exclusive and predestined fate of the illegitimate. Human beings have a heartening habit of coping better with difficulties as time goes by and a sort of pool of knowledge and experiences develops to which they can refer.

While writing this book, I have been editing another one about one parent families. The overwhelming impresssion created by the experiences of contributors to that book is the amazing adaptability and courage of men and women who are, for all sorts of reasons, the sole supporters of their children. They are aware of the problems and the disadvantages and they wage a largely cheerful and effective battle against them. It is very difficult to believe that all those children are destined to become disturbed, educationally inadequate and socially disadvantaged. It is equally difficult to assert that the children of two parents are always comparatively advantaged. In fact, the very presence of a husband or a wife lulls some parents, makes them less acutely aware of the dangers and problems inherent in the family situation *per se*. Ultimately, of course, it is the quality and not the quantity of parents that matters, and I see no reason to assume that the lone father is not every bit as acceptable and potentially successful as the lone mother.

There is a slight temptation to argue that if two parents are better than one, then a single female must be better than a single male. This assumption is based not so much on prejudice as on unquestioned habit. Sex seems to be a curiously crude and inaccurate way of measuring parental effectiveness. Not all women make good mothers, or even want to be mothers. Some men, on the other hand, can be excellent, caring and capable fathers – by which I suppose we must understand biologically male 'mothers'. At a time when women are asserting their right to be freed from the traditional proscriptions imposed upon their sex by virtue of their biological potential for motherhood, it would be foolish to assume that men are congenitally incapable of taking over the hitherto exclusively female business of child-raising. Some men have already exchanged roles with their wives. Others, among whom I would include myself, do so on an occasional, planned basis. We are not frustrated, incapable or mad. We do encounter prejudice, receive unwanted and unmerited sympathy and are frequently patronized. None of this, however, detracts from the pleasure we derive from or our effectiveness in discharging the tasks. Of course, it is very much easier for those of us who are married, but if a single woman can be expected to survive with a child, so can a man. As long as he can provide the normal ingredients of home and care – which must inevitably entail state grants, more day-care centres etc. – there is no reason why his sex and the habits of society should prevent any man from truly fathering his children.